DEFICIT

WHY SHOULD I CARE?

Second Edition

Marie Bussing-Burks

Apress

Deficit: Why Should I Care? Second Edition

ISBN-13 (pbk): 978-1-4302-4839-2

ISBN-13 (electronic): 978-1-4302-4840-8

Trademarked names may appear in this book. Rather than use a trademark symbol with every occurrence of a trademarked name, we use the names only in an editorial fashion and to the benefit of the trademark owner, with no intention of infringement of the trademark.

President and Publisher: Paul Manning
Acquisitions Editor: Jeff Olson
Technical Reviewer: Todd Knoop
Editorial Board: Steve Anglin, Mark Beckner, Ewan Buckingham, Gary Cornell, Louise Corrigan, Morgan Ertel, Jonathan Gennick, Jonathan Hassell, Robert Hutchinson, Michelle Lowman, James Markham, Matthew Moodie, Jeff Olson, Jeffrey Pepper, Douglas Pundick, Ben Renow-Clarke, Dominic Shakeshaft, Gwenan Spearing, Matt Wade, Tom Welsh
Coordinating Editor: Rita Fernando
Copy Editor: Judy Ann Levine
Compositor: SPi Global
Indexer: SPi Global
Cover Designer: Anna Ishschenko

Distributed to the book trade worldwide by Springer-Verlag New York, Inc., 233 Spring Street, 6th Floor, New York, NY 10013. Phone 1-800-SPRINGER, fax 201-348-4505, e-mail orders-ny@springer-sbm.com, or visit www.springeronline.com.

For information on translations, please contact us by e-mail at info@apress.com, or visit www.apress.com.

Apress and friends of ED books may be purchased in bulk for academic, corporate, or promotional use. eBook versions and licenses are also available for most titles. For more information, reference our Special Bulk Sales–eBook Licensing web page at www.apress.com/bulk-sales.

The information in this book is distributed on an "as is" basis, without warranty. Although every precaution has been taken in the preparation of this work, neither the author(s) nor Apress shall have any liability to any person or entity with respect to any loss or damage caused or alleged to be caused directly or indirectly by the information contained in this work.

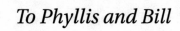

To Phyllis and Bill

Contents

About the Author

Marie Bussing-Burks holds Master of Business Administration and Doctorate of Arts in Economics degrees. She is an Assistant Professor of Economics in the College of Business at the University of Southern Indiana.

Bussing-Burks is the author of six other books: *100 Years of the Federal Reserve: The Central Banking System in the United States, Starbucks: Corporations that Changed the World, Money for Minors: A Student's Guide to Economics, Influential Economists, Profit from the Evening News: Using Leading Economic Indicators to Make Smart Money Decisions,* and *The Young Zillionaire's Guide to Taxation and Government Spending.* In addition, she has more than 30 magazine, newspaper, and journal articles to her credit.

About the Technical Reviewer

Todd Knoop is a Professor of Economics and Business at Cornell College and the author of two books: *Recessions and Depressions: Understanding Business Cycles* and *Modern Financial Macroeconomics: Panics, Crashes, and Crises*. He also has a forthcoming book on financial markets in emerging market economies and has published articles in the *Canadian Journal of Economics*, *Economic Inquiry*, and *Southern Economic Journal*. He holds a Doctorate from Purdue University.

Acknowledgments

Writing this book has been a great learning experience and a collaborative effort. It is with sincere appreciation that I acknowledge the efforts of those who assisted me in this endeavor.

A special thanks to Jeff Olson, Executive Editor/Business at Apress, for providing me with this enlightening opportunity to explore the deficit and the national debt. His knowledge and insight on business topics has been invaluable. My sincere gratitude to Rita Fernando, Coordinating Editor at Apress. Her guidance, expertise, and contributions assisted me greatly. I am grateful to Professor Todd Knoop for his helpful comments on review of the text. My thanks to Cathy Bowman for her excellent editorial assistance. Last, I owe a debt of gratitude to Harry Zeeve, the National Field Director of The Concord Coalition, and Representative Bill Frenzel, guest scholar at Brookings Institution, for their valued interview responses.

It has been a pleasure working with everyone who has assisted with the writing of this book. I appreciate the assistance in investigating the largest economic concern of the time: the rising deficits and $16 trillion plus national debt.

Introduction

The United States is experiencing a host of serious economic problems, including soaring unemployment, stagnant production, a crippled housing market, and ballooning government spending. Although each issue is important, it is the government's burgeoning spending, along with the weakening economy from an approaching "fiscal cliff," that has really captured everyone's attention. The hot economic topic discussed around the kitchen table, at dinner parties and business meetings, on nightly news programs, and in academic settings is the deficit and the national debt.

Most people agree that the government is a big spender and the mounting debt is troublesome. In fact, in a recent USA Today/Gallup poll, federal government debt and terrorism tied as the most serious issue of concern to Americans for the future well-being of the United States. Yet some people, including prominent economists, are not all that worried about the debt.

In the press, on the Internet, and in the media, the public is often misinformed regarding the specifics of the current deficit and debt issue. In fact, the terms deficit and debt are routinely and incorrectly used as interchangeable vocabulary. This book will set the record straight on the deficit and the debt, while presenting the facts in a clear, concise manner.

Here is a preview of what you will learn. The federal government's annual budget impacts the national debt. If the government were to post a balanced budget, it would mean the government's revenues equal expenses, or that taxation and fee collection are equal to spending. A balanced budget is an extremely rare occurrence. Routinely, budgets are either in a surplus or a deficit. When the government spends less than it collects in taxes, it runs a surplus. Each year for a 4-year period from 1998 to 2001, the United States had a surplus budget. Since then, the government has incurred a widening and alarming deficit.

The deficit is the yearly amount by which government spending exceeds taxation. The yearly deficit for 2012 is projected to surpass $1 trillion. The deficit stirs concern and debate because the government must borrow funds to pay for its excess spending. Too large to place on a giant credit card, the funds are borrowed by the federal government by issuing Treasury securities and savings bonds. The total amount of borrowing, known as the *national debt* (sometimes referred to as the *federal debt* or *public debt*), has topped $16 trillion. To picture just how large the debt figure is, envision $16 followed by

12 zeros—$16,000,000,000,000. Another way you can think of it is going into debt for $16 billion, and doing this one thousand times.

Who owns this enormous amount of debt? About $4.7 trillion of the total is held by U.S. government agencies, such as the Social Security Administration and government trust funds. The government borrows the other $11.3 trillion from the public, which includes individuals, businesses, banks, state and local governments, and foreign entities. Foreign creditors have recently played a part in the debt debate. Increased reliance on foreign countries—like China, our largest creditor nation with holdings of more than $1 trillion in U.S. Treasury securities—has caused anxiety to some.

The amount of debt held by the public mirrors the amount of the nation's wealth that has been assumed by the federal government to finance total federal spending from prior years. When a cash deficit exists, the government must borrow. When a cash surplus exists, the funds can be used to pay down the debt held by the public.

It's important to note that the federal government does not get free use of this money. The government must pay for the use of funds by offering a rate of interest that is attractive to its investors. Each year, there is a line item in the federal budget for interest, an expense for which we receive no current productive value. In 2011, the government paid $454 billion for the use of the funds. It is possible that the issuance of new debt might put upward pressure on interest rates and consequently, interest payments.

Calculating the national debt takes a simple math formula. Add up all the deficits (negative numbers), and then add in the few surpluses, and you get the national debt—the total amount of Treasury and savings bonds outstanding. So each year that the government incurs a deficit, the debt will increase. As noted, this habit of deficit spending has resulted in more than $16 trillion in U.S. debt to this point.

The government debt has risen over the years, experiencing especially dramatic growth spurts during wartimes (due to high defense spending) and during recessions. When the country is experiencing tough economic times, work is not as plentiful, business profits falter, and the government receives less money from taxpayers. At the same time, the government is spending more money than usual on welfare programs, social initiatives, and aid to the unemployed. This widening gap between spending and revenue makes the deficit grow.

In December 2007, the United States entered a recession, or a general slowdown in the economy. The government, in an effort to help the economy, paid for many new stimulus programs designed to create jobs or bolster the safety net for its citizens. The goal of dampening the recession and improving economic growth has caused the recent deficits and debt to rise.

The public debt—and controversy about it—has been with us for some time. The Bureau of the Public Debt notes its first recorded debt in 1791, at just over $75 million to honor the Revolutionary War obligations. The debt shrank to zero by January 1835, but soon sprang into the millions again. Rising and falling over the years, it was in 1982 that the debt topped $1 trillion. Since hitting this marker, it has been a wild ride on the debt roller coaster.

Now let's fast-forward to look at the growth over the past decade. At the turn of the century, the national debt stood at just under $6 trillion and the country sported a slight surplus. The official fiscal 2011 national debt total clocked in at $14,790,340,328,557.15, and the yearly deficit at a whopping $1,299,595,000,000. The fiscal year 2012 (ending September 30) will have total debt over $16 trillion and a deficit between $1.1 and $1.3 trillion. According to the Treasury Department's *Annual Report on the Public Debt*, the debt is estimated to hit $19.6 trillion by 2015. The federal government has borrowed roughly 40 percent of its total budget for the past several years, a trend that could leave the United States in an economic crisis.

Increasing interest payments, the debt burden to your children and grandchildren, and an increased reliance on foreign creditors are just a few of the foreseen problems.

On the other hand, there are positive aspects of deficit spending, too. Government spending provides needed goods and services to our economy; deficit spending supports fiscal policies during times of need; and Treasury securities are useful instruments to support a strong monetary policy.

In reading this book, you will learn to think like an economist who must weigh the pros and cons of an issue. In particular, you will learn to sharpen your economic skills and decide, after reading the facts, whether deficits and the debt will lead to economic ruin and anarchy; a stronger economy that will, over time, allow us to pay down the debt before disaster strikes; or something in between. Here is a sneak peek:

Chapter 1, Crash Course on the National Debt: This chapter delves into the role of the government in the U.S. economy. The government must provide certain essential goods and services for its taxpayers. In turn, the government collects taxes to pay for these goods and services. But when the government spends more than it takes in, a deficit occurs, and the government must borrow to pay for its overspending. The federal budget process begins each year in February, when the president submits his budget request to Congress. Congress then debates, amends, and takes action on the budget (see Figure 1-1). On October 1, the government's fiscal year begins. This chapter takes a look at the budget process and the different types of budgets: balanced, deficit, and surplus. You will learn the correct definitions of *deficit* and *national debt*, and see how each is calculated.

Figure I-I. President Barack Obama and Vice President Joe Biden meet with Jack Lew, Office of Management and Budget Director, and Rob Nabors, Director of Legislative Affairs, on April 5, 2011, in the Oval Office. The President and Vice President later met with House Republican and Senate Democratic leaders to discuss ongoing budget negotiations. On Friday, April 8, 2011, President Obama announced a last-minute budget deal that averted a partial government shutdown which was scheduled to occur at midnight. *Source: Office White House, photo by Pete Souza.*

- *Chapter 2, A Huge Credit Card:* This chapter introduces the history of the debt and the issuing agency, the Bureau of the Public Debt. It examines details of the agency's financing instruments, Treasury securities and savings bonds. These outstanding securities total the national debt, so learning the particulars is important. Other main topics include the ownership of the debt, United States versus foreign, and interest payments, which hamper the government's ability to balance the budget. Get a glimpse into the recent unparalleled growth of the deficits and the debt.

- *Chapter 3, Primer on the Current Global Economy:* This chapter investigates our interconnected economies. We live in an economy that is global; therefore, what happens elsewhere can and does affect the United States. In a global economy, financial markets and product markets are highly integrated. Check out the economies of Portugal, Ireland, Italy, Spain, Greece, and China and uncover some potential impacts on the U.S. market.

- *Chapter 4, Deficit and Debt Projections:* This chapter describes how the government's spending and tax policies influence output. The government has historically used fiscal policies to alter the macro economy, with some successes and some failures. We will look at an overview of recent fiscal policies, including the economic stimulus package designed to combat the December 2007 downturn, and the impacts on the deficit and debt. This chapter introduces the rising debt compared with gross domestic product (GDP), considers the productive capacity debate, and provides projections on the debt trend.

- *Chapter 5, Do Deficits and the Debt Matter?:* This chapter sets the stage for the debt debate. The broad dispute over the deficit and the national debt has been stirring for years. A notable historic point dates back to the Depression era, when Franklin Roosevelt took over in 1932 as a four-term president (1933–1945). FDR instituted a number of different programs, such as Social Security, welfare reforms, new banking controls, and the New Deal programs, in an effort to restore the economy. Although FDR ran some modest deficits, he refused to run up huge deficits, which were essential to end the Great Depression.

  It was back in 2002, at a meeting of President Bush's economic advisors, that Vice President Dick Cheney said, "Deficits don't matter," a viewpoint many politicians and economists have held for years. The deficit at that time was just $158 billion. Now some in Congress and many interest groups say deficits matter a great deal, and we must eliminate deficits and pay down the debt. In early 2009, as many citizens became concerned with hefty government spending, self-organized groups began sprouting, using the Tea Party name as a basis for their political platform. The Tea Partiers believe in limited government, fiscal restraint, and lower taxes; and they have held Tea Party rallies to protest excessive government spending.

- *Chapter 6, Deficits Do Not Matter:* This chapter focuses on the viewpoint that deficit spending is not a concern to the health of the U.S. economy. In fact, sometimes running a deficit contributes beneficial effects for the economy. Government spending supports the economy through building strong economic growth and more jobs. The federal government's deficit financing provides many essential services to society, such as national defense, education, public welfare, Social Security, Medicare, and Medicaid. In addition, the government sells Treasury securities and savings bonds to finance the debt. Not only are these important savings instruments for investors, but the Federal Reserve formulates monetary policy using government securities.

A common view says that Treasuries can be issued continually to finance the government's needs, and it is not imperative to pay down the debt. Furthermore, a popular way to measure the deficit level, deficits to GDP, shows declining numbers on the horizon. Many other countries are in a similar deficit spending mode, planning to ride out the global downturn. The United States is not unique in its deficit situation.

- *Chapter 7, Deficits Do Matter:* This chapter explores the concerns with deficit financing. It provides a deeper explanation as to why some feel the debt matters more now than it has in the past. You will be introduced to both the long-time arguments against deficit financing—burden to future generations, hefty interest payments, crowding out of the lending, and economic instability—along with some new twists. The United States has an increased reliance on foreign creditors. China is now our number one creditor. In addition, many feel that the U.S. government is setting a bad example of fiscal irresponsibility for its citizens.

- *Chapter 8, Get a Handle on the National Debt:* This chapter teaches the reader about government spending and ways to curb deficit spending. Pork projects impact government money spent in a particular locale and brings advantages to their political representatives. Fundamental reform of Social Security, Medicare, and Medicaid programs will be highlighted as options to aid the debt drain. The chapter also provides an overview of the debt ceiling (currently $16.4 trillion), and the pros and cons of raising it.

- *Appendix A, Voice Your Opinion on the Debt:* This appendix provides readers with simple but important take-charge options. The public can make contributions to help pay down the debt, become educated taxpayers, submit ideas to their congressman, and exercise their right to vote. If you want to make an impact and be heard, this appendix is a must-read.

- *Appendix B, Web Sites for Debt and Deficit Information:* This appendix lists resources to check out for current, up-to-date information about the debt and deficit. A host of government agency web sites, economic think tanks, and academic sites are available. This is a complex problem, so be sure to have access to the sources that can provide current information as the various issues emerge.

- *Appendix C, Political Party Views of the Debt:* This appendix explores the plans of both major parties, Republicans and Democrats, to reduce the debt and deficit. Each party has expressed grave concern over the lack of a fiscal plan and compromise which will be required to place the country on sound footing. Take a look over the past 50 years to see what our presidential administrations have done regarding taxes, spending, and the deficit situation.

Business professionals, parents, retirees, and students are all talking about the debt. This quick read will not only get you in the conversation, but will place you at the top. *Deficit: Why Should I Care?* explains the implications of the single biggest economic concern of our time: the burgeoning $16 trillion national debt and accompanying record-breaking deficits. Once you understand the basics of the deficits, you will have the information you need to make up your own mind and decide if you should care about the deficit.

Crash Course on the National Debt

Just as in a household, the U.S. federal government operates on an annual budget. While households spend money on food, clothing, and shelter, the U.S. government spends money on big items such as roads, defense, and education. If a household spends more than it earns each year, it must borrow money or dip into savings, if available; so does the government. When it spends more than it takes in through taxes and other revenues, a deficit occurs and it must borrow money. This chapter explores budgeting, deficits, surpluses, and debt—government style.

Government-Provided Goods and Services

You are touched by services provided by the U.S. government on a daily basis. Did you send or receive a letter today through traditional mail? Then you used the services of the U.S. Post Office. Did you travel on a highway? Chances are you used the nation's federal road system. Did you take any prescription medicine? If so, the medicine you took is regulated by the U.S. Food and Drug Administration. Did you buy or sell stock? If you did, that transaction was monitored by the U.S. Securities and Exchange Commission. One of the many roles of the U.S. government is to provide citizens with essential goods and services—usually the types of things average individuals are unable to provide for themselves. Providing the goods and services we all have come to expect requires the U.S. government to spend money ... a lot of money.

There are three levels of government in the United States: local, state, and federal. Each level specializes in making unique purchases that are difficult or impossible for the average citizen to make. Local governments spend on services such as education, police and fire protection, and public transportation. State governments spend on education, public welfare, health care, hospitals, and highways. The federal government spends on such big-ticket items as national defense, transfer payments (such as Social Security and Medicare), various grants to state and local governments, and interest payments on the national debt, which, along with the deficit, is the focus of this book.

Unlike most state and local governments, which must balance their operating budgets year in and year out, the federal government historically spends more than it takes in from taxes, and this practice is what creates a budget deficit. As you can see in Figures 1-1 and 1-2, according to the President's proposed Budget of the United States Government, Fiscal Year 2013 (at the time of this writing the FY 2013 official budget has not been passed), the federal government will spend $3.8 trillion during the fiscal year, yet collect only $2.9 trillion in taxes and receipts, resulting in a deficit just under $1 trillion.

■ **Note** The U.S. government runs on a fiscal year, not a calendar year like the rest of us. The federal government's fiscal year begins October 1 and runs through September 30.

Before I discuss the deficit and debt in more detail, let's drill down and take a look at U.S. government revenues and expenditures. Where is the federal government getting this $2.9 trillion? Take a look at the top three revenue generators in Figure 1-1. The largest source of revenue for the federal government in 2013 is individual income taxes, estimated at over $1.3 trillion. This is tax paid on personal income. At around $677 billion, the second largest source of receipts is Social Security payroll taxes, a tax on employees and their employers to fund the Social Security program. Number three, corporate income taxes—a tax levied on corporate profits—weighs in at approximately $348 billion.

Federal Receipts, Fiscal Year 2013

Proposed Budget (in billions of dollars)

Receipts (What the Government Takes In)

Individual income taxes	$1,359
Corporation income taxes	$348
Social insurance and retirement receipts:	
Social Security payroll taxes	$677
Medicare payroll taxes	$214
Unemployment insurance	$58
Other retirement	$10
Excise taxes	$88
Estate and gift taxes	$13
Customs duties	$33
Deposits of earnings, Federal Reserve System	$80
Other miscellaneous receipts	$21
Total receipts	**$2,902**

Figure 1-1. Federal receipts, 2013. *Source: Budget of the U.S. Government, FY 2013, Table S-5, "Proposed Budget by Category."*

Now look at the spending side of the budget, in Figure 1-2. Of the $3.8 trillion in outlays, the top three expenditures are substantial. Appropriated programs—money set aside for a specific purpose, such as defense, regulation, highways, and so forth—is the top expediture at an estimated $1.3 trillion, which amounts to just over one-third of all spending. The second largest expected outlay, listed under mandatory spending, rings in at $820 billion. It is Social Security, the federal program of social insurance for the elderly and disabled. Medicare, a federal health insurance program for those aged 65 and over (or under 65 and physically disabled), at approximately $523 billion, takes the number three spot for expected spending.

Federal Spending, Fiscal Year 2013

Proposed Budget (in billions of dollars)

Outlays (What the Government Spends)

Appropriated ("discretionary") programs	$1,261
Mandatory programs:	
Social Security	$820
Medicare	$523
Medicaid	$283
Troubled Asset Relief Program (TARP)	$12
Other mandatory programs	$654
Net interest	$248
Disaster costs	$2
Total outlays	**$3,803**

Figure 1-2. Federal spending, 2013. *Source: Budget of the U.S. Government, FY 2013, Table S-5, "Proposed Budget by Category."*

Based on the proposed presidential budget, the deficit for fiscal year 2012 will be $901 billion. This means that the U.S. government will spend just under $1 trillion more than what it earns in revenue. How does the government pay for its deficit spending? By selling government bonds. These annual deficits, as you will see, all contribute to the national debt. Today's national debt, at over $16 trillion, is the total of all accumulated deficits less any surpluses.

Financial Management, Government Style

Another role of the U.S. government is financial management. This large responsibility includes levying taxes, borrowing funds when necessary, and preparing a budget.

The U.S. government has a financial master plan—a budget—that enables it to implement and maintain government programs and deliver services. How does it go about financing its expenditures? Government expenditures are financed through revenues, largely taxation, and government borrowing.

Taxing

Most government spending is financed via taxation. According to the 16th Amendment to the U.S. Constitution, ratified in 1913, Congress is authorized to tax personal and business income. It is worth noting that among all U.S. government receipts, personal income tax, at nearly 43 percent of the total, contributes most to the income of our government. The government is thus able to fund a substantial part of its programs—but not all—through the tax base.

DEBT GLOSSARY

- *Government deficit:* The fiscal-year dollar amount by which government spending exceeds government receipts. When a deficit occurs, the government must borrow.

- *National debt:* The total dollar amount of outstanding government securities; represents accumulated government deficits less accumulated government surpluses.

The federal tax on individual and business income is referred to as a *progressive tax.* Another name for this is *graduated tax.* A progressive tax is one in which the tax rate goes up as the tax base increases. In other words, the more money individuals and businesses make, the greater percentage they pay in taxes. The theory is that high-income individuals and businesses should pay a greater amount of taxes proportionally, especially during economically prosperous eras. It puts more of the tax burden on the wealthy than on lower wage earners.

Borrowing

If the government spends more than it takes in through taxes, it becomes a borrower. The U.S. government borrows to cover the deficit by issuing Treasury securities (debt instruments often just called "Treasuries"). With a national debt exceeding $16 trillion, the United States is the biggest borrower on the globe. Your share of the national debt is roughly $50,000 at the time of this writing, and it is rising each second. This means that every man, woman, and child in the United States—all 314 million of us—would have to write a check for $50,000 to wipe out the national debt.

What is the process for budgeting trillions of dollars? And why does the U.S. government, in most years, accept that it will have a deficit that in turn will contribute to the national debt? Read on.

Budgeting

You must understand how the federal budget is prepared to fully comprehend the government's financial situation. Each February, the president submits to Congress a proposed budget, which is prepared for the president by the Office of Management and Budget (OMB). Congress then debates the budget and, in September, passes a budget resolution. On October 1, the federal government's fiscal year begins. Targets for revenue and spending (and as a result, surpluses and deficits) are set. The president can either sign or veto the entire budget bill.

The budget can be divided into two different types of spending, discretionary (aka, appropriated) and mandatory, the distinction being how the funds are allocated by Congress.

The discretionary budget, which is just over one-third of federal spending, is set by Congress, which must decide on the level of spending for discretionary programs in a given year. A discretionary program must go through the annual appropriations process each year. Types of discretionary programs include national defense, education, housing assistance, highways, and foreign aid.

Mandatory spending comprises roughly two-thirds of the federal budget. Mandatory spending has been authorized by law and is the result of legislation enacted previously. The major part of this spending is for entitlement programs—payments that individuals are entitled or guaranteed to receive, based on certain qualifications such as age, income, or military status. The largest mandatory program is Social Security, which will continue to expand as the "baby boomer" population ages, putting a huge strain on the health of the U.S. economy. Medicare, the government's health insurance coverage for people aged 65 years and older (or under 65 and disabled), is the second largest mandatory program. Again, as the baby boomer population ages, the federal government will have rising Medicare expenditures, adding more long-term financial pressure.

Another mandatory program, Medicaid, jointly funded by the federal and state governments, provides health insurance to low-income individuals. It is the third largest mandatory spending category. Interest on the national debt is also a mandatory spending category. This is money that must be paid to those who buy Treasuries, which includes investors in the United States and abroad, and the central banks of foreign countries. It is the U.S. central bank, the Federal Reserve, that is the largest buyer of Treasuries. As of September 5, 2012, the Fed held $1.6 trillion in Treasury Securities, pumped up as part of two rounds of QE, or quantatative easing, beginning in 2008. The efforts were designed to stimulate the economy by buying bonds to keep long-term interest rates low.

As Figure 1-2 showed, mandatory spending, at over $2 trillion, is a big reason the U.S. budget doesn't balance and creates a deficit. Shouldn't it be easy to close the gap? As a matter of practicality, there are only two ways to reduce the deficit—increase the amount of revenue (for example, by collecting more taxes) and/or cut spending. The more controversial debate centers on the potential necessity to adjust the promises made to people receiving or planning to receive Social Security and Medicare. Let's look at an overview of each of these programs and some of the promises made.

Problem Area: Social Security

The Social Security Act was signed into law by President Roosevelt in 1935. It was designed as a social insurance program as an after effect of the depression, the intent being to safeguard against poverty in the elderly population (see Figure 1-3). Social Security provides retirement benefits, plus family (dependents), survivor, and disability programs.

MORE SECURITY FOR THE AMERICAN FAMILY

THE SOCIAL SECURITY ACT AS AMENDED OFFERS GREATER OLD-AGE INSURANCE PROTECTION TO PEOPLE NOW NEARING RETIREMENT AGE.

SOCIAL SECURITY BOARD

Figure 1-3. The Great Depression was the most severe economic crisis in modern times, causing unemployment to exceed 25 percent. Franklin D. Roosevelt promised economic security for the elderly, signing the Social Security Act in 1935. Social Security has grown to be the largest U.S. government mandatory spending program. *Source: Courtesy of the Franklin D. Roosevelt Presidential Library and Museum, Hyde Park, New York.*

This system is a "pay as you go" system, which means that taxes are collected from current workers to pay for people currently receiving Social Security benefits. This was not a problem in the early years of the system. At the beginning, the number of workers paying into the system was far higher than the number of people receiving benefits. In 1950, there were 16.5 workers per beneficiary.

Social Security is the major source of income for a majority of senior citizens. In fact, according to the Social Security Administration, nine out of ten people aged 65 and older receive Social Security benefits. In 2011, over 55 million Americans received $736 billion in benefits.[1]

After World War II, there was an explosion in the number of births, referred to as the "baby boom." The baby boomers are the group of people born between 1945 and 1964—in the United States, 76 million people were born during that span. As of 2011, the oldest individuals in that group are now 65, and the rest will eligible to begin receiving Social Security benefits over the next 20 years. Baby boomers can't get full Social Security benefits until they turn 66 (1945–1959) or 67 (1960–1964), but eligibility is on a graduated scale and will not necessarily begin on their birthday.

By 2036, the population of older individuals is expected to almost double, from 41.9 million today to 78.1 million. Today there are 2.9 workers to each Social Security beneficiary. In 2036, current projections show, there will be just 2.1 workers to each Social Security beneficiary.[2] As the ratio of workers per retiree continues to fall, it is questionable whether the government will be able to fulfill its obligations.

In addition, due to better health care and medicine, people in the United States are living longer than ever before. This, too, puts greater strain on the Social Security system. When Social Security was in its early stages in 1940, the average life expectancy of a 65-year-old was near 14 years. Today the life expectancy of a 65-year-old is close to 20 years.[3] People now have more years of retirement and more time to collect Social Security. To keep up with this trend in life expectancy, Congress has increased from 65 to 67 the age at which a person is eligible to collect benefits. This begins with individuals born in 1938 or later, and gradually rises until it hits 67 for those born after 1959.

Currently, the Social Security system collects more in payroll taxes (FICA taxes) than it pays out to beneficiaries. Workers pay 6.2 percent of their wage income, up to $106,800, an amount that is matched by their employers.

---

[1]Social Security Administration. *Fast Facts and Figures about Social Security*. Available at www.ssa.gov (accessed September 10, 2012).
[2]Ibid.
[3]Ibid.

The excess money goes into an account called the Social Security Trust Fund. Money that goes into the trust fund is invested in U.S. government securities. At the end of 2011, this trust fund held $2.7 trillion in securities.[4] The government has placed securities in the trust fund earmarked for Social Security, but it has spent the money on other goods and services. By 2015, it is expected that the Social Security Trust Fund will shift from a surplus to a deficit.

To take funds out of the Social Security Trust Fund to deal with the deficits, the government must pay back the securities being held by the trust fund as well as the interest due. The financial drain will be so huge that there are only a few available choices to deal with this issue: raise taxes, cut spending, increase the payroll tax for Social Security, and/or reduce Social Security benefits.

Problem Areas: Medicare and Medicaid

As mentioned earlier in the chapter, Medicare is a federal program that provides health insurance coverage to people aged 65 or over, or under 65 with disabilities. Medicaid is a joint federal and state program, administered by the state governments, to provide health insurance to low-income people and families. The fiscal concerns about these programs is that with continued increases in the U.S. population, people living longer, and the number of medical procedures available, these programs are going to place an unbearable drain on the government budget in years to come. It is a problem because these health care entitlement programs have already been promised.

In 2012, Congressional Budget Office (CBO) baseline projections show the federal government will have net outlays of $486 billion for Medicare, with the amount rising to $884 billion by 2022. These obligations are a debt owed by the federal government. For the same 10-year period, CBO baseline projections for the Medicaid program show 2012 net outlays of $258 billion, with the amount rising to $622 billion by 2022—more than doubling in 10 years.

The deficit persists in part due to the federal government's spending habits, both mandatory and discretionary. Although it may not be wise for society to eliminate entitlement programs, there are a number of approaches available to reduce mandatory spending. Several options are highlighted in Chapter 8, including extending the retirement age to receive full Social Security benefits. Priorities must be set for annual discretionary spending, with adjustments to entitlements. Deficits will not go away until we as a nation adjust our spending patterns or increase revenue.

---

[4]Board of Trustees. *The 2012 Annual Report of the Board of Trustees of the Federal Old-Age and Survivors Insurance and Federal Disability Insurance Trust Funds*, April 25, 2012, Washington, DC: Government Printing Office. Available at www.ssa.gov (accessed September 10, 2012), p.14.

BUDGET GLOSSARY

- *Budget deficit:* A situation in which government spending exceeds its revenue during a given period of time.

- *Budget surplus:* A situation in which government spending is less than its revenue during a given period of time.

- *Balanced budget:* A situation in which government spending is exactly equal to its revenue during a given period of time.

The Budget Equation: Receipts less Outlays

The current debate over the government budget boils down to the gap between spending and receipts, which has been widening over the past few years—and not in a good way. Although government spending has increased in recent years, the tax and revenue stream has not kept up.

The budget equation is very simple. When government outlays are higher than receipts, a budget deficit exists. When the receipts are higher than the outlays, the result is a budget surplus. A balanced budget, in which receipts exactly equal outlays, is an extremely rare occurrence. When the government spends more than it takes in through taxes during a fiscal year, it "runs a deficit." Adding all the yearly deficits together, less any yearly surpluses, results in the national debt figure. So financing the government deficit each year forces the debt upward. Over the past few years, the U.S. budget has revealed some harrowing deficit numbers, surpassing the $1 trillion mark, partially because of recent changes in fiscal policy (see Table 1-1).

Table 1-1. Summary of Receipts, Outlays, and Surpluses or Deficits (in millions of dollars)

	Receipts	Outlays	Surplus or Deficit (–)
2000	$2,025,191	$1,788,950	$236,241
2001	$1,991,082	$1,862,846	$128,236
2002	$1,853,136	$2,010,894	-$157,758
2003	$1,782,314	$2,159,899	-$377,585
2004	$1,880,114	$2,292,841	-$412,727
2005	$2,153,611	$2,471,957	-$318,346
2006	$2,406,869	$2,655,050	-$248,181
2007	$2,567,985	$2,728,686	-$160,701
2008	$2,523,991	$2,982,544	-$458,553
2009	$2,104,989	$3,517,677	-$1,412,688
2010	$2,162,724	$3,456,213	-$1,293,489
2011	$2,303,466	$3,603,061	-$1,326,948

Source: Budget of the U.S. Government, FY 2013, Historical Tables, Table 1.1, "Summary of Receipts, Outlays, and Surpluses or Deficits: 1789–2017."

At the time of this writing, the United States has a national debt over $16 trillion. As mentioned, the debt equals all accumulated deficits less any accumulated surpluses. When a deficit occurs, it increases the national debt. The budget for fiscal year 2011, for example, increased the national debt by approximately $1.3 trillion.

Deficits and Business Cycles

Yet another role of the federal government is to stabilize the economy, which may at times involve increasing the deficit. The macroeconomic objectives of the government are to encourage economic growth, minimize inflation, and spur employment. The U.S. government attempts to contribute to a strong U.S. economy through the execution of economic policies. The government has two main choices—fiscal policy and monetary policy.

Fiscal policy, implemented by the president and Congress, is the adjustment of taxation and/or government spending to influence the overall economy. *Monetary policy* is employed by the Federal Reserve Bank ("the Fed"), which manipulates the money supply, interest rates, and availability of credit to affect the health of the U.S. economy. The strategies that both the Fed and Congress use to achieve macroeconomic objectives are hotly debated, and I detail the methods and the arguments in later chapters. But regardless of how you feel about the policy tools, it is advisable not to view the policies singularly. Often the two strategies are utilized together to best achieve economic goals. An advantage of monetary policy is that it can assist in improving the economy without increasing the deficit. An important component to a strong economy is to have sound monetary and fiscal policies.

The government also has powerful tools, called *automatic stabilizers*, to provide the economy with an automatic boost. An automatic stabilizer is government spending or taxing that automatically rises or falls with economic activity. For example, as personal income rises, so do income taxes. There are many economists who favor the use of automatic stabilizers over fiscal policy. Automatic stabilizers are a form of nondiscretionary fiscal policy because they do not require any specific actions by government. The reason is that stabilizers change automatically, based on economic conditions. They are built into the structure of the system. It is a government expenditure or revenue that responds countercyclically by moving in the opposite direction of the current economic cycle. There is no need for approval from Congress or the president to go forward with this type of economic policy and consequently no policy lags.

Unemployment insurance and welfare are two major programs that are automatic stabilizers; they increase or decrease automatically to offset current economic conditions. Here's an example of how it works. In a recessionary economy, many people lose their jobs, causing unemployment compensation to rise. So government expenditures increase automatically during recessions. The unemployment payments allow people to spend money they would not otherwise have, thereby injecting money into the spending stream during an economic downturn. Consequently, unemployment compensation helps people maintain a somewhat similar spending stream as prior to losing their jobs. Because this group of people is still out in the economy spending, this automatic stabilizer helps minimize the impact of job losses and makes the cyclical downturn less severe.

When the economy is in a recessionary period, welfare payments also rise. Again, this is an automatic increase in government spending in response to worsening economic conditions. It is a countercyclical action, injecting new money into the system during a down time. Based on previously written entitlement rules, people must meet specific qualifications for both unemployment and welfare. So when the economy is booming again, fewer people will be in need of unemployment and welfare, reversing the cycle.

Income tax is also an automatic stabilizer. During a recession, for example, income falls and individuals fall into a lower tax bracket. Because of the progressive tax system, people pay a decreasing portion of income tax as income falls. People now have more funds available to spend on disposable purchases. This provides a stimulating impact for the economy and lessens the impact of a recession. Conversely, when the economy is strong people will find themselves making more money and moving into a higher tax bracket. Due to the progressive nature of the tax system, people will pay additional taxes on their higher incomes. People now have less cash to spend on disposable purchases, and this will slow down the economy. Once again, it is a countercyclical action.

December 2007 Recession

Recessions and the national debt have a definite connection. During a weak economy, deficits tend to grow. Rising deficits, in turn, aggravate the growing debt burden. As you can see in Table 1-1, over the past decade the country has run a deficit every year since 2002. The Business Cycle Dating Committee of the National Bureau of Economic Research (NBER), a private, nonprofit, nonpartisan research organization centered in Cambridge, Massachusetts, identified December 2007 as the beginning of the most recent downturn in the economy. This recession has caused the deficit to burgeon, making the deficit and debt a hotly debated topic.

During the recession, economic activity declined, causing tax revenue to decline. This further widened the spread between revenue and expenditures, and the country ended up with huge deficits over the past few years.

Budget deficits typically increase during recessions because tax revenue goes down and government spending rises. In this case, the government responded to the economic situation with the $787 billion American Recovery and Reinvestment Act of 2009; assistance for the financial, housing, and automotive industries; and an extension of unemployment benefits. These actions were all designed to pump up the economy, but they also further expanded the deficit by increasing spending.

The Business Cycle Dating Committee has determined that the end of the recession, a trough in business activity, occurred in June 2009. The December 2007 to June 2009 recession lasted 18 months and was the longest recession since World War II. According to the Business Cycle Dating Committee, "In determining that a trough occurred in June 2009, the committee did not conclude that economic conditions since that month have been favorable or that the economy has returned to operating at normal capacity. Rather, the committee determined only that the recession ended and a recovery began in that month."[5]

Clearly, the Business Cycle Dating Committee notes this is not a robust expansion and many people do not yet feel relief. It is a modest expansion at best. Revenue growth is further restrained by the Tax Relief, Unemployment Insurance Reauthorization, and Job Creation Act of 2010. The modest uptick in any economic activity will be countered by this $858 billion act, which includes, among many items, an extension of the Bush Administration's tax cuts, advantageous tax rates for long-term capital gains and dividends, and favorable estate tax laws.

What level and type of fiscal stimulus programs are appropriate to move a country out of a recession? During a recession, deficit spending may boost aggregate demand and recharge the economy. Government spending and tax cuts can increase business activity and create job opportunities. Such programs can also lead to deficits and mounting debt. Also, fiscal policies occasionally fail to work effectively in stimulating demand, yet the debt remains. The controversy over fiscal programs and their impact on curing a recession are discussed in coming chapters.

In the next chapter, you will learn how the government borrows the additional funds that it needs to operate. It is not a new story; in fact, borrowing by the federal government dates back to 1791. You will learn about the Treasury agency that funds the debt, the Bureau of the Public Debt. Who holds the big credit card for the U.S. government? If you own a U.S. Savings Bond—perhaps

---

[5]National Bureau of Economic Research. "Business Cycle Dating Committee, National Bureau of Economic Research report, September 20, 2010." Available at www.nber.org/cycles/sept2010.html (accessed April 25, 2011).

given to you as a birthday or graduation gift—you own a piece of the federal debt. I will also explore details of the other debt instruments—Treasury bills, notes, bonds, and Treasury Inflation-Protected Securities. Are you interested in the top U.S. creditors—China, Japan, and the "oil exporting countries"? Read on for more details. You will also get a peek at the monumental interest payments the U.S. government is making—an additional cost of deficit spending.

A Huge Credit Card

In the introduction, I mentioned that the national debt was far too large to put on a traditional credit card. But as this chapter will show, the U.S. Treasury and its agencies allow the country to spend and borrow, much as an individual with a wallet full of credit cards.

The U.S. Constitution gives Congress the power to borrow money on the credit of the United States. The U.S. Department of the Treasury ("the Treasury") issues or creates the debt, but it's the duty of a Treasury agency—the Bureau of the Public Debt—to borrow the money needed to operate the federal government and account for the debt. The Bureau of the Public Debt has the task of managing the debt, including selling the debt, making payments to debt holders, and keeping administrative records. Its official headquarters is in Washington, DC, with the primary operations and computer center located in Parkersburg, West Virginia.

Financing the federal government is largely accomplished by selling government bonds. These include Treasury bills, notes, bonds, Treasury Inflation-Protected Securities (TIPS), and U.S. Savings Bonds, and occasionally war bonds to help finance war efforts. As you will see, much of our federal debt has been incurred to pay for wars throughout our country's history.

History of the Debt

The Bureau of the Public Debt was organized in 1789. In fact, the Bureau of the Public Debt notes its first recorded debt in 1791, at just over $75 million to honor Revolutionary War obligations.[1] It was founding father, economist, and statesman Alexander Hamilton who believed in a strong central government and rallied for the government to take on some debt to help meet its expenses. He said, "A national debt, if it is not excessive, will be to us a national blessing."[2] Hamilton was the chief architect of the U.S. Treasury Department, and was named the young nation's first Secretary of the Treasury.

The debt shrank to zero by January 1835, but soon sprang into the millions again. It was during the Civil War period that the country saw the debt skyrocket. In 1860, the year before the Civil War began, the debt level was approximately $65 million, and by the year following the war, 1866, the debt had grown to $2.7 billion.

The end of World War I in 1918 brought with it a hefty bill for the payment of the war efforts, and the debt hit $27 billion in 1919. The cost of World War II multiplied the debt fivefold, from $51 billion in 1940 to $258 billion in 1945. The Korean War in the early 1950s caused only a modest uptick in the debt, but enough to ignite concerns about the problems associated with paying for defense spending. The Vietnam War saw larger increases of the debt, rising to near $382 billion by 1970.

It was in 1982 that the total federal debt topped $1 trillion, and by the year 2000—despite a few years in the late 1990s in which the deficit disappeared and the country ran a budget surplus—it had risen to six times that figure. With the historic September 11, 2001, terrorists attacks on New York, Pennsylvania, and Washington DC, economic progress was thwarted and spending escalated for homeland security and the wars in Iraq and Afghanistan. The U.S. economy went into a downturn, and President George W. Bush authorized tax rebates and tax cuts during this time to propel the economy, and the debt kept growing. In December 2007, the United States entered a particularly tough recession. President Obama fired back quickly with a $787 billion stimulus program to encourage economic recovery, bringing the debt to topple $16 trillion at the end of fiscal 2012. (That figure includes the portion held by the government.)

Think Like an Economist

Do you want to think like an economist? Economists are particularly interested in the portion of debt that is held by the public. When the total federal

---

[1]Bureau of the Public Debt. "Our History." Available at www.publicdebt.treas.gov/history/history.htm (accessed February 6, 2011).
[2]TreasuryDirect Kids. "The History of U.S. Public Debt: The Beginning of U.S. Debt." Available at www.treasurydirect.gov/kids/history/history.htm (accessed February 6, 2011).

debt is reduced by the portion held by government agencies, it is called debt held by the public. To provide a truer picture of rising debt values, Table 2-1 shows the real, inflation-adjusted rise in the debt (in FY 2010 dollars) held by the public, post-WWII. According to these values, in 1946 the federal government owed approximately $2.3 trillion to creditors who had loaned the government money to fund past deficits. This number has risen over the past 64 years to reach over $9 trillion at the end of 2010. It is projected to shoot up to over $13 trillion in 2015.

Table 2-1. Debt Held by the Public in 2010 dollars

Fiscal Year	FY 2010 Dollars (in billions)
1946	2,276.4
1950	1,677.3
1955	1,525.0
1960	1,414.9
1965	1,456.9
1970	1,315.5
1975	1,349.2
1980	1,683.0
1985	2,716.2
1990	3,721.8
1995	4,900.7
2000	4,268.2
2005	5,109.8
2010	9,018.9
2015	13,243.5 (estimated)

Source: *Office of Management and Budget, Analytical Perspectives, Budget of the U.S. Government, Fiscal Year 2012, Table 6-1, "Trends in Federal Debt Held by the Public."*

Liberty Bonds

Although government bonds of various types have been offered by the Bureau of the Public Debt throughout its history, some of the patriotic bond issues are the most memorable. When the United States was preparing to enter World War I, Liberty Bonds were introduced and purchasing them became a symbol of patriotism by U.S. citizens. The funds from the sale of the bonds were used to support the Allied cause in WWI and help pay for the war. Later, the face value of the bonds was paid back, plus interest.

A series of four Liberty Bonds were issued by the government during 1917 and 1918. Each issue was authorized by the government to print and sell a set dollar amount of the bonds. The first Liberty Bond met with a rather unenthusiastic response, so the Bureau of the Public Debt launched the second bond with a carefully planned publicity campaign. Famous artists created posters to advertise it, and movie stars hosted Liberty Bond rallies. Boy Scouts and Girls Scouts sold the bonds in their communities, and Army pilots even traveled around the country doing airplane stunt shows in an effort to sell more bonds. Buying the bonds was promoted as being the duty of all U.S. citizens. Many of the posters, such as the one shown in Figure 2-1, prominently feature the Statue of Liberty in the background, and they have become collectible and historic symbols of American patriotism. The second issued Liberty Bond sold $3 billion in bonds at 4 percent interest, redeemable after 10 years.

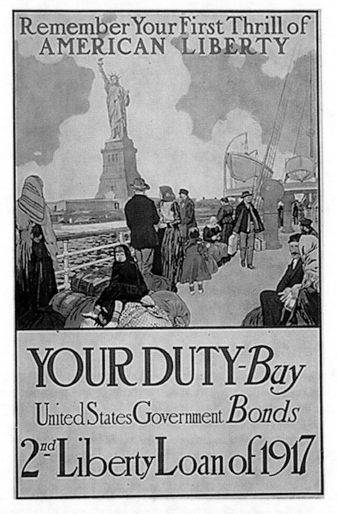

Figure 2-1. A poster encouraging the sale of government bonds for the second issue of Liberty Bonds, "Liberty Loan of 1917" (ca. 1917–1919). *Source: The National Archives and Records Administration.*

War Bonds

Many investors were disappointed with their investment in Liberty Bonds. Values fell on the Liberty Bonds, and some investors had to sell the bonds at significant losses. So the U.S. government tried a different approach with the next war, which was to be a much more expensive undertaking. World War II came in at an estimated cost for the United States of $323 billion. The Bureau of the Public Debt was heavily involved because roughly $211 billion of the total amount was borrowed money.

Much of the borrowing was in the form of nonmarketable debt, or U.S. Savings Bonds (also called War Bonds). Savings Bonds were first offered on March 1, 1935, and the promotion and sale of bonds associated with the war was very successful. Savings Bonds were different from Liberty Bonds because they were nonnegotiable (not transferable from one party to another), registered, and had fixed values. This was great for the small investor because the bonds could easily be turned into cash.

The poster shown in Figure 2-2—"Bonds Build Ships! Buy More Bonds"—was only one of many that stressed the responsibility of the public to buy bonds to provide financial assistance for fighting WWII. The United States relied on its citizens to help with wartime funding. The advertising campaign turned out to be a successful strategy because it made investors feel secure and gave them a strong feeling of patriotism by helping their country. It truly was an appeal for help because the bonds offered rates that were lower than could be acquired elsewhere. The War Bonds were zero-coupon bonds (which are sold at a discount and are redeemed at full face value), selling for 75 percent of their face value, in denominations ranging from $10 to $100,000. At first they were called Defense Bonds, but when the Japanese attacked Pearl Harbor on Dec 7, 1941, the name appropriately changed to War Bonds. In the end, 18 percent of the total U.S. debt for the war was funded by War Bonds.

Figure 2-2. A poster used to promote the purchase of government bonds for the wartime effort (1941–1945). *Source: The National Archives and Records Administration.*

Who Owns the Debt?

The system of selling Treasury securities and bonds to finance the U.S. debt is a highly organized process. As previously stated, the U.S. Treasury issues the debt, and the Bureau of the Public Debt manages the debt. The current Bureau of the Public Debt Commissioner, Van Zeck, aptly explains the agency's role: "In a nutshell, we borrow by selling Treasury bills, notes, bonds, TIPS, as well as savings bonds; we pay interest to investors; and, when the time comes to pay back the loans, we redeem investors' securities. Every time we borrow or pay back money, it affects the outstanding debt of the United States."[3]

Neither the U.S. Treasury nor the Bureau of the Public Debt makes the decisions on how the borrowed funds are spent; Congress decides how the money is allocated. The *debt ceiling* is the cap that Congress imposes as the maximum amount of debt that the government may have outstanding. When the limit is reached, the Treasury must stop borrowing until Congress raises the limit.

Public Debt

The debt is divided into two main categories: debt held by the public and intragovernmental holdings (see Table 2-2). The public, which holds roughly 70 percent of the debt, includes individuals, businesses, pension funds, insurance companies, mutual funds, banks, state and local governments, and foreign entities.

Table 2-2. Total Public Debt Outstanding As of August 31, 2012

Category	Amount (in millions)	Percentage of Debt
Debt held by the public	$11,122,282	69.81%
Intragovernmental holdings	$4,810,953	30.19%
Total public debt outstanding	$15,933,235	100.00%

Source: Bureau of the Public Debt, Debt Position and Activity Report, August 2012.

Government Debt

As indicated in Table 2-2, the remaining 30 percent of the total public debt outstanding is held by U.S. government agencies and trust funds, such as the Social Security Administration, Federal Housing Administration, Postal Service Fund, Highway Trust Fund, and Federal Disability Insurance Trust Fund. These government accounts are among those that accumulate cash above and beyond current needs, to pay for future obligations. Cash surpluses are generally invested in Treasury debt. Note that interest paid on debt owed by one government account to another does not have a net effect on government spending.

[3]Bureau of the Public Debt. "Commissioner's Welcome." Available at www.publicdebt.treas.gov/whoweare/welcome.htm (accessed February 8, 2011).

Marketable vs. Nonmarketable Obligations

Debt largely is issued in the form of Treasury securities, including Treasury bills, notes, bonds, Treasury Inflation-Protected Securities (TIPS), and Savings Bonds. The bulk of Treasury securities—bills, notes, bonds, and TIPS—are marketable because they can be bought and sold in the secondary market after they are purchased from the Treasury. These Treasury securities are considered *liquid* because they are traded frequently. Savings Bonds are referred to as nonmarketable securities because they are registered to a specific owner. They cannot be transferred to other people by market sales.

Treasuries and Savings Bonds are generally considered stable and safe investments. Interest on these issues is exempt from state and local taxes but is subject to federal tax. All issued government bonds are backed by the full faith and credit of the U.S. government. Because of the safety advantage, rates and yields on all government obligations tend to be relatively low. As Table 2-3 shows, the average rate for marketable and nonmarketable obligations is under 3 percent.

Table 2-3. Marketable Debt vs. Nonmarketable Debt As of August 31, 2012

Category	Amount (in millions)	Percentage
Marketables	$10,607,347	66.57%
Nonmarketables	$5,325,887	33.43%
Average interest rate		2.621%

Source: Bureau of the Public Debt, Debt Position and Activity Report, August 2012.

Marketable Securities

Treasury bills, Treasury notes, Treasury bonds, and Treasury Inflation Protected Securites are referred to simply as Treasuries. Although many similarities do exist among these instruments, such as liquidity and a wide secondary market, there are unique differences such as risk and maturity. The U.S. government sells a variety of instruments, to suit investor preferences, to finance the debt. Read on to learn more details.

Treasury Bills

Treasury bills (called "T-bills" for short) are the government's short-term securities, in that they mature in 1 year or less. Typical instruments are 4-, 13-, 26-, and 52-week bills. These are also known as 1-month, 3-month, 6-month, and 1-year bills. Banks and financial institutions tend to be the largest purchasers of Treasury bills. Highly liquid, many investors see T-bills as the least risky investment on the market. Consequently, T-bills generally carry a low rate of interest, even compared to Treasury notes and bonds.

T-bills are unique Treasury instruments. They do not pay interest but are sold at a discount from face value. T-bills are sold in denominations of $100, and the maximum purchase is limited to $5 million. A purchaser pays less than face value (also called *par amount*) at the time of purchase, but receives face value once the T-bill matures. Investors make money on the spread between the discount price and the face value. Technically, these instruments do not pay interest. Often this is referred to as *implicit interest*.

For example, assuming you bought a 1-year T-bill for $980 and its face value was $1,000, you would earn $20 at the end of the term. The implicit interest can be determined according to the following formula:

$$(\text{Face value} - \text{Price})/\text{Price} = \text{implicit interest.}$$

For this simple example, $20/$980 is a 2.04 percent implicit interest.

T-bills can be bought directly from the U.S. Treasury or indirectly through banks, brokers, and dealers. They are auctioned electronically every week. There are two ways to bid on bills, either competitively or noncompetitively. Competitive bidders must go through a bank, broker, or dealer, and can't buy more than 35 percent of the initial offering amount. Noncompetitive bidders are limited to $5 million in T-bills. Here's how it works.

With a noncompetitive bid, the bidder agrees to take the discount rate or yield determined during the auction. The benefit is that the bidder is guaranteed to receive the full amount of the bid.

With a competitive bid, the bidder names the discount rate or yield, but has to wait to see if they are a winning bidder. If the bidder's rate is less than or equal to the high discount rate or yield calculated during the auction process, the bidder gets the T-bill. But if the bidder's rate is over the auction rate, the bidder won't be able to purchase any T-bills.

The T-bill rate is commonly used as an index for other loans, such as business and consumer loans. As interest rates change according to underlying economic conditions, so does the T-rate. An adjustable rate loan might be tied to the T-bill rate, with a few percentage points commonly added to the T-bill rate. So, for example, an adjustable rate loan might be the T-bill rate plus three points. Therefore, when the rates on T-bills go up, so do many other loan rates.

Treasury Notes and Bonds

Similar to the nickname for Treasury bills, Treasury notes are called T-notes and Treasury bonds are called T-bonds. T-notes earn a fixed rate of interest every 6 months until the note matures. Notes have a maturity from a minimum of 1 year up to a maximum of 10 years. Current note issues are 2, 3, 5, 7, and 10 years. T-bonds carry a maturity longer than 10 years, currently issued with a term of 30 years. Notes and bonds are sold monthly or quarterly, depending on the maturity of the issue. When the note or bond reaches maturity, the holder receives the face value.

Notes and bonds are sold in increments of $100, with a minimum purchase of $100. In a single auction, an investor can buy up to $5 million in notes or bonds by noncompetitive bidding, or up to 35 percent of the initial offering amount by competitive bidding (bidding is described in the preceding section, "Treasury Bills").

The price of a T-note or bond may be greater than, less than, or equal to its face value. A good rule of thumb to remember is that when interest rates rise, bond prices fall. When interest rates fall, bond prices rise. Thus, bond prices and interest rates are inversely related. Here is simple example. Assuming you own a $1,000 bond paying 3 percent interest, every year you will receive a $30 interest payment (or $15 every 6 months). Now further assume that new bonds coming to market of similar quality and maturity pay 4 percent. The new bonds will provide a $40 interest payment annually, making your 3 percent bond look less attractive. If you want to sell it, the price of your bond will have to fall below its $1,000 par value to increase the interest rate. On the other hand, if coupon rates fall and new bonds are selling at a 2 percent rate, your 3 percent bond looks great because it is paying $30 a year, and will consequently sell over its par value.

Interest rates for T-notes are typically higher than rates for T-bills. Interest rates for T-bonds are generally higher than rates for T-notes. Yield curves are traditionally upward sloping, meaning that the longer the term, the higher the interest rate premium. The market rewards investors for committing their funds for a longer period of time because there is a great deal of uncertainty in the market that may translate into volatility in the value of the security. The economy faces global crises, political situations, inflation, output problems, and employment issues that can impact the marketplace. Investors generally want to be compensated for longer use of their funds because of potential risks long term.

There is also a large secondary market for trading T-notes and T-bonds, so they are considered to be highly liquid (easily turned into cash). Liquidity also reduces risk since holders can usually sell U.S. government securities easily if need be.

BOND BASICS

If interest rates rise, bond prices fall.

Interest Rates	*Bond Prices*
⇧	⇩

If interest rates fall, bond prices rise.

Interest Rates	*Bond Prices*
⇩	⇧

To place a noncompetitive bid, you may bid through the Treasury directly, or use a bank, broker, or dealer. To place a competitive bid, you must use a bank, broker, or dealer. When you bid competitively, you specify the yield you want, but this does not mean that you will get the bid. With a noncompetitive bid, you take whatever yield is determined at auction.

Treasury Inflation-Protected Securities (TIPS)

As with T-notes and T-bonds, TIPS pay interest every 6 months and return the principal on maturity. These were first issued in 1997 to protect investors from inflation. If you think traditional treasuries are safe, these might be described as super-safe. What makes TIPS different from normal T-notes and T-bonds is that the return and principal are automatically adjusted for inflation. The principal is tied to the Consumer Price Index (CPI), an inflationary indicator that measures the change in the cost of a fixed market basket of goods and services. Therefore, if inflation rises, so does the principal. If inflation falls, so does the principal. TIPS do have a set interest rate and pay interest every 6 months. But because the rate is paid on principal, the interest rises if the principal increases and falls if the principal falls.

When the TIPS reaches maturity, the holder receives the greater of the inflation adjusted principal amount or its original par value. The terms can be 5, 10, 20, or 30 years. You can buy from the U.S. Treasury, a bank, or broker. They tend to carry very low interest rates because they carry inflation protection. Risk is consequently lower. You can hold the TIPS until it reaches its full value, or sell it before maturity in the secondary market.

Nonmarketable Securities: Savings Bonds

Unlike Treasury securities, which have a wide secondary market, U.S. Savings Bonds are nonmarketable securities. This means they are sold and registered to a specific owner and cannot be traded with other investors. As with Treasuries, Savings Bonds are considered extremely safe because they are backed by the full faith and credit of the U.S. government. Like all Treasury securities, Savings Bonds are exempt from state and local taxes, but, unlike other Treasury securities, all federal taxes may be deferred until the Savings Bond is redeemed. Savings Bonds are registered so they can be replaced if they are lost or stolen. Two types of Savings Bonds are currently available, Series EE and Series I Savings Bonds.

Series EE Savings Bonds

Series EE Savings Bonds pay a fixed rate of interest, which does not fluctuate during the life of the bond. These types of bonds can be purchased as electronic bonds or paper bonds. You can buy them in paper form from banks, or in electronic form from the U.S. Treasury. Either way, the bond earns interest each month for 30 years. In both the electronic and paper versions, you cannot buy more than $5,000 face value of bonds during any calendar year. Paper Series EE Bonds may be bought in denominations of $50, $75, $100, $200, $500, $1,000, $5,000, and $10,000. Electronic Series EE Bonds may be purchased in amounts of $25 (the minimum) or any amount up to $5,000.

If you purchase a paper Series EE Bond, you pay half the face value. For example, a $25 investment purchases a $50 bond. The bond continues to rise in value, and interest is added to the principal. When the bond matures, the holder gets the accrued interest plus the purchase price of the bond. On the other hand, you pay face value when you purchase electronic Series EE Bonds, so a $50 bond costs $50. But you will be paid full value for the bond when it matures. You receive interest electronically.

Series I Savings Bonds

Like Series EE, Series I Savings Bonds are available electronically or in a paper version. The intent of the security is to protect investors from inflation. These bonds are sold at face value with a maturity of 30 years. The earnings rate consists of a combination fixed rate that does not change, plus a rate connected to the CPI, or Consumer Price Index—an inflation measure. Simply speaking, if the inflation rate rises, then the interest rate goes up. Conversely, if the inflation rate falls, so does the interest rate on the bond. Generally considered very low risk, Series I Bonds protect the earning capacity of the bond and rise during periods of inflation. For both paper and electronic purchases, the limit is a $5,000 maximum purchase in one calendar year. Electronic purchases can be made in amounts of $25 or more up to $5,000. Paper bonds sell in $50, $75, $100, $200, $500, $1,000, and $5,000 amounts.

Foreign Investors

As the U.S. debt burgeons, the nation continues to rely on foreign sources for financing. As you can see from Table 2-4, as of June 2012, foreign investors held $5,292.3 billion, or $5.3 trillion, of U.S. Treasuries. This is roughly 48 percent of total privately held debt.

Table 2-4. Top Ten Major Foreign Holders of Treasury Securities (in billions of dollars; holdings at end of period)

Country	June 2012	June 2011
China, Mainland	$1,164.3	$1,307.0
Japan	$1,119.3	$881.5
Oil exporters	$261.3	$242.6
Brazil	$242.8	$216.2
Caribbean banking centers	$240.2	$216.2
Taiwan	$191.9	$146.6
Switzerland	$165.7	$118.1
Russia	$157.8	$151.7
United Kingdom	$139.1	$135.7
Hong Kong	$135.5	$112.4
Grand total for all countries	$5,292.3	$4,690.6

Source: Department of the Treasury/Federal Reserve Board (August 15, 2012).

The amount of the U.S. debt held outside of the United States is at an all-time high. China, Japan, and the "oil exporters" are the top foreign creditors. China, although tapering off purchases during the year, is still the largest foreign buyer of U.S. debt. Japan, the second largest holder of Treasury debt, has increased its position significantly over the last year rising to 27 percent. The "oil exporters" is a powerful entity, growing its Treasury holdings 8 percent during that year. The exporting countries include Ecuador, Venezuela, Indonesia, Bahrain, Iran, Iraq, Kuwait, Oman, Qatar, Saudi Arabia, the United Arab Emirates, Algeria, Gabon, Libya, and Nigeria.

The largest foreign holder of U.S. Treasury securities, China, currently holds $1,164.3 billion in American debt. This means that it holds roughly 10.5 percent of the debt held by the public. Foreign holdings of Treasury securities have increased fivefold from where they stood in 2000 at $1,038.8 billion, which was just over 30 percent of the total privately held debt.

So you can see a trend of increasing numbers of Treasury securities held by foreign countries and international investors. Foreigners want a portion of the U.S. debt because they are dollar-denominated IOUs, currently considered a safe haven. Another issue to contemplate is the cost of using these funds, which means sending interest payments abroad, as discussed in the next section. This money also ends up in the hands of people outside of U.S. borders, rather than in the hands of someone in the United States. On the positive side, the massive purchases of Treasuries by foreigners have kept interest rates at low levels, a cheap form of financing for the United States. However, it places the country under increased reliance on the foreign sector to finance the deficit spending of the United States.

Interest Payments

Each dollar that the U.S. government borrows, either domestically or from foreign creditors, carries an interest cost. As the total amount of debt increases, there is a constantly growing interest expense on that debt. One of the impacts of deficit financing and rising debt is that the government must fund the interest expense each year.

Estimated spending for net interest outlays on the debt in fiscal year 2012 totaled $241.6 billion. This is a 17 percent increase from fiscal 2011, which tallied net interest of $206.7 billion. Net interest is calculated as the interest paid to holders of Treasury debt issues less interest received by government trust funds. It is affected by both interest rates and the amount of debt outstanding. To put these numbers into perspective, note that the entire budget receipts for 2012 are estimated to total $2.6 trillion. That means the country spent roughly 10 percent of everything taken in during the year just on interest costs.

Here are a few more numbers to put this in perspective. Net interest was the sixth largest U.S. government outlay by function. Money spent on Social Security in 2012 was the highest outlay, at $767.1 billion. National defense was next at $737.5 billion, followed by income security at $554.3 billion, Medicare at $492.3 billion, and health at $373.8 billion. You can see in Chart 2-1 that interest is a big part of the government's budget, about 6 percent of the total. Looking at it another way, the entire cost of interest on the debt at $241.6 billion could cover the combined spending outlays for Veterans Affairs at $125 billion, Transportation at $105 billion, and Disaster Relief and Insurance at $11 billion.

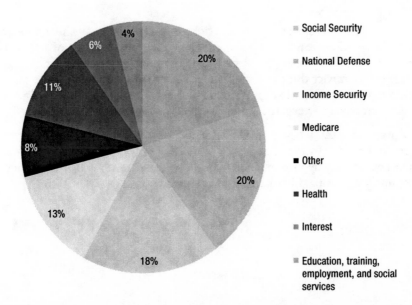

Legend:
- Social Security
- National Defense
- Income Security
- Medicare
- Other
- Health
- Interest
- Education, training, employment, and social services

Pie chart values: 4%, 6%, 20%, 11%, 8%, 20%, 13%, 18%

Chart 2-1. Federal Outlays by Function, 2012. *Source: Budget of the U.S. Government, FY 2013, Historical Tables, Table 3.2, "Outlays by Function and Subfunction:1962–2017."*

At month end August 2012, interest rates were down. The average rate (excluding TIPS) for marketable debt was 1.443 percent, the average rate for nonmarketable debt was 3.638 percent, and the overall rate was 2.587. When rates start to return to higher levels, the federal interest cost will increase dramatically. Interest expenses also are projected to keep growing dramatically as the U.S. debt increases. The Treasury anticipates interest on the net public debt to grow to $653.6 billion by 2015.

Summary

The United States has been borrowing money to operate the federal government since 1791. A staggering amount of money is needed to run the United States, and the Bureau of the Public Debt is the government agency that sells and manages the debt. There are a number of ways to borrow from the public—marketable securities such as T-notes, various bonds and bills, TIPS, and nonmarketable securities such as those from the Savings Bond program.

Who owns this public debt? A lot of U.S. citizens, banks, and institutions, as well as the foreign sector, have purchased securities over many years to fund our government. Every dollar that is borrowed carries an interest cost—the cost of doing business with these people, institutions, and foreign governments.

The federal government has many functions in our society. One such function is to stabilize our economy, when necessary, such as in times of economic turmoil or war. Fiscal policy involves the adjustment of government spending or taxation to impact the economy. The government characteristically cannot stabilize the economy and keep the budget intact. One of the effects of a fiscal policy is that it usually creates a deficit, which pushes up the total debt.

In the next chapter we will investigate our increasingly complex, interconnected world. We live in a global economy where product markets and financial markets are highly intergrated. Read on to see how a major policy shift in one country can impact economies around the world.

Primer on the Current Global Economy

We have already established that the U.S. $16 trillion debt is number one on the economic fix-it list. But economies have become increasingly connected; we live in an economy that is global. Therefore what happens elsewhere can and does affect the United States. We cannot focus only on our own nation's financial picture. In a global economy, financial markets and product markets are highly integrated. This means the European debt crisis or China's trade slowdown can stress U.S. markets. And with 24-hour news coverage, world policies—such as strict austerity measures in Greece—and events, like the recent two-level downgrade of Italy's debt, can have an immediate impact on the U.S. economy.

Our Interconnected World

On July 17, 2012, the words of Federal Reserve Chairman Ben Bernanke could be heard around the globe. In a 2-hour testimony before the Senate Committee on Banking, Housing, and Urban Affairs, Bernanke gave his semiannual report on the state of the economy. According to the powerful Federal Reserve chief, ongoing problems in Europe and the fiscal situation in the United States are the two biggest risks to U.S. recovery. Bernanke explained our integrated economies, saying, "Europe's financial markets and economy remain under significant stress, with spillover effects on financial and economic conditions in the rest of the world, including the United States."[1]

While Bernanke indicated Europeans have the incentives and resources to resolve their crisis, he also encouraged U.S. financial firms to manage the risks associated with their exposures to Europe. Bernanke encouraged Congress to come up with a credible medium-term plan to shrink the deficit to avert a financial crisis. U.S. stock markets dipped during Bernanke's speech and continue to fluctuate constantly with news concerning the European financial crisis.

Economies around the world are intertwined like domino pieces. Once you tip the first piece, it is difficult to stop the chain of events. The global economy functions in a similar manner. A major policy shift or notable event in one country can tip economic towers around the world.

The debt crisis began in Greece several years ago and spread to Ireland, Portugal, Spain, and finally, Italy. The weakening of the European economy has had a domino effect, touching even the world's fastest-growing economy of China and causing it to slow. Why? A major reason is that China's biggest export market is the European Union. With the European debt crisis, employment problems, and declining individual income, China's exports to these countries are down. And the dominos likely will continue to tumble to other Asian countries, which trade heavily with China.

The Impact of Weakening Economies

Much of the world is still recovering from the 2007–2009 recession, sometimes referred to as the "Great Recession." Many countries have never recovered and are being ravaged even further. Most European countries are in a negative growth cycle and Portugal, Greece, and Spain are all in recession. Italy is in a double-dip recession. Ireland just missed a recession call due to an output revision. These five countries, sometimes referred to as PIIGS (Portugal, Italy, Ireland, Greece, and Spain), are nations in severe debt and financial crisis, and the domino effect they are spreading is technically referred to as financial contagion. Financial contagion simply means a financial problem in one country that spreads or impacts other countries. The risk of these countries spreading their financial contagion across the globe is serious. The excessive debt to GDP numbers will be analyzed in Chapter 7, but needless to say the

---

[1]Ben S. Bernanke, *Semiannual Monetary Policy Report to the Congress*, speech delivered before the Committee on Banking, Housing, and Urban Affairs, U.S. Senate, Washington, DC, July 17, 2012, http://www.federalreserve.gov/newsevents/testimony/bernanke20120717a.htm (accessed July 23, 2012).

economic climate of these countries presents the threat of a global downfall. The rock of economic strength and second-largest global economy, China, is showing signs of a slowdown.

Potential Global Recession

Is the world in a global recession? That is not an easy question to answer because there is no generally accepted definition of a global recession. It is often thought of as a prolonged world downturn, a period of economic decline on a global perspective, or a widespread financial meltdown. Although most economists concur on 2012 that we are not in a true global recession, and signs of a world recovery lurk, there are also strong indicators that the scales could be easily tipped to a world-wide downturn. Major risks to the global economy do exist and are being heavily impacted by the European sovereign debt crisis, so fiscal reforms must continue.

The International Monetary Fund (IMF) benchmarks 3 percent year-over-year economic growth or below to indicate a global recession. World growth was 3.9 percent for 2011, and the IMF projects world output at 3.5 for 2012, and 3.5 for 2013.[2] GDP growth across Organisation for Economic Co-operation and Development (OECD) countries—"First World" nations—is projected to slow to 1.6 percent in 2012, and tick up to 2.2 percent in 2013.[3]

Trade Downturns

World trade also has taken a downturn. World trade growth is expected to decline for the second year in a row, according to the World Trade Organization (WTO). It is projected to slow to 3.7 percent in 2012; this from 5 percent trade growth in 2011, and trade growth of 13.8 percent in 2010.[4] Trade was held back in 2011 due to a number of shocks, including the European debt crisis, severe flooding in Thailand, and the Japanese earthquake and tsunami. Europe is a major trading partner with the United States and the financial crisis has negatively impacted the United States; the flooding in Thailand has made it difficult to obtain technology parts, and because Japanese plants account for roughly 12 percent of world car production, the earthquake and tsunami have made it difficult to obtain some cars.

---

[2]International Monetary Fund, "World Economic Outlook Update, July 16, 2012," Available at www.imf.org (accessed July 30, 2012).
[3]Organisation for Economic Co-operation and Development. Economic Outlook 91, Press Conference, Paris, May 22, 2012. Available at www.oecd.org (accessed July 30, 2012).
[4]World Trade Organization. 2012 Press Releases/658, April 12, 2012, World Trade 2011, Prospects for 2012. Available at www.wto.org (accessed July 25, 2012).

Let's take a look at positive and negative economic points of the European countries where the trouble originated. We also check in on China, where trouble is brewing.

Portugal

Negative:

- Severe recession, and it may grow even worse.

- Unemployment has reached 15 percent.

- GDP contracted 1.6 percent in 2011, and the IMF predicts it will contract 3.3 percent for 2012.

- Painful austerity plans, including pay cuts for public jobs. Tax increases have provoked riots.

- Outlook on sovereign debt rated negative by S&P and Moody's.

- Received a €78 billion ($111 billion) bailout from the EU/IMF.

Positive:

- The country's 10-year bond yields dropped from 17 percent to over 10 percent—an affirmative sign of a level of confidence in the economy.

- IMF notes the difficult euro economic environment, but hails Portugal for sticking to their target for budget execution.

Ireland

Negative:

- Outlook on sovereign debt rated negative by S&P and Moody's.

- Received an €85 billion ($108 billion) bailout rescue package from EU/IMF.

- Bailout package from EU/IMF carries high interest cost— more than Portugal and Greece—because it is tied to market rates.

- May require a second bailout due to losses in the banking system.

Positive:

- GDP shrank by 1.1 percent in the first quarter of 2012 but grew 0.7 percent in the fourth quarter of 2011. Previous estimate was a 0.2 percent contraction, which would have resulted in a recession.

- In late July 2012, the country returned to a degree of normal routine and sold government bonds after a 2-year sabbatical.

- The country hopes to be the first nation to emerge from the debt crisis.

- EU leaders agreed to possibly improving terms of the bailout.

Italy

Negative:

- Double-dip recession.

- Concern over ability to service massive debt.

- Strict and widely unpopular austerity measures.

- On July 12, 2012, Moody's downgraded Italian debt two levels, from A3 to Baa2, expecting the country's GDP to decline 2 percent during 2012.

- Unemployment rate exceeds 10 percent.

Positive:

- Bond yields have fallen slightly, lowering the price the country has to pay to borrow funds.

Greece

Negative:

- The country has been in a recession since 2009.

- Credit agencies downgraded Greece's debt rating in late 2009. S&P and Moody's classify debt in C categories— signaling substantial risk.

- The economy shrank 6.9 percent in 2011.

- Already into its second bailout.

- Unemployment rate exceeds 24 percent.
- Public outrage and riots occurring over severe austerity measures.
- Greece unable to deliver and asks deadline for austerity measures be moved from 2014 to 2016.

Positive:

- Greece's main industry of tourism remains fairly strong and is forecast to grow.

Spain

Negative:

- Recession is deepening.
- Rates for borrowing rising to excessive levels, a sign that investors are questioning the ability of the country to pay back its debt.
- European leaders granted an emergency loan package to bail out banks.
- GDP shrank 1.5 percent in 2010, 0.6 in 2011, and Spain's government predicts the economy will continue to shrink until 2014.
- S&P rates the outlook as negative and Moody's is under review—both rate bonds in the lower medium grade category.
- Unemployment rate rises above 24 percent.
- Austerity measures have touched businesses and consumers.

Positive:

- Officials maintain that the country will not need a bailout.

China

Negative:

- Real estate housing bubble potentially ready to burst.
- Housing downturn could force China into a recession.

- Economic slowdown in Europe is expected to further slow Chinese growth (see Figure 3-1).

Figure 3-1. Secretary of State Hillary Rodham Clinton and U.S. Secretary of the Treasury Timothy F. Geithner held a press conference in Beijing, China, following the conclusion of the U.S.–China Strategic and Economic Dialogue on May 25, 2010. China's top trading partner is the European Union, followed by the United States. *Source: U.S. Department of State.*

- GDP growth was 10.3 percent in 2010, and dropped to 9.5 percent in 2011. IMF is projecting a GDP growth rate of 8 percent for 2012 and 8.5 for 2013.
- Debt remains from a recent stimulus program.

Positive:

- Second largest economy in the world.
- World's largest exporter.
- Strong ratings from S&P and Moody's.
- Largest international holder of U.S. debt.
- China is stepping up their stimulus program at local levels to counter the slowdown.

World Financial Markets

The health of Europe's banks, particularly in the troubled countries of Portugal, Ireland, Italy, Greece, and Spain, has become a major area of concern.

Unresolved Banking Crises

The banks are in a serious situation where they need substantial recapitalization to survive. U.S. banks have been preparing and have already significantly reduced their exposure in these countries. Banks in the United States have billions of dollars in European exposure through a number of different means including sovereign bonds, European businesses, and bank deposits, along with other claims such as derivatives, guarantees, and credit commitments.

Bank of America has been cutting its exposure to Portugal, Ireland, Italy, Greece, and Spain. Their total exposure to these five countries was $16.6 billion on December 31, 2010, but fell to $15.3 billion by December 31, 2011.[5] Bank of America has been selling assets and curtailing loans. Other large banks, such as JP Morgan Chase and Citigroup, have reduced their exposure in Europe as well. But many banking players in the game have not been so proactive. If these troubled countries do not fix their banking system, a liquidity crunch—a lack of lendable funds—could shock the entire global economy.

Stock markets in most major countries are interconnected and highly correlated as well. When markets drop, it is a bad sign because it leads to a drop in economic activity. The European debt crisis has had a negative impact on the U.S. stock market, with news of sky-high deficits, recessions, and ballooning unemployment rates leading the news. The U.S. and world markets are tuned in to news from Europe 24 hours a day for updates in the fiscal drama. Consumers and businesses become skittish based on what they hear, hold off on spending, and this drags the economy further down.

Declining Income and Jobs

As seen previously, problems affecting the global economy are widespread and interconnected. On top of the list is high unemployment and declining income. At the simplest level, to generate income for a tax base, and in turn pay off the deficit, people must be employed. Employment will bring economic growth and prosperity to the world. The International Labour Organization (ILO) in its Global Employment Trends 2012 report, says the number one priority for countries is to create more jobs. The fiscal austerity measures are having a negative impact on the job market. The ILO finds the global job market situation troublesome, and the trends are especially of concern in Europe, where the unemployment rate has risen in the majority of the countries since 2010. The U.S. labor market recovery has stalled, and the unemployment rate has

---

[5]Bank of America. Form 10-k for fiscal year ended December 31, 2011 (p. 13). Available at www.sec.gov (accessed July 30, 2012).

been hovering in the 8 percent range. Even in China, a better-educated working age population is searching for employment.[6] The world needs to create about 50 million jobs to reach the pre-2008 crisis level of jobs. According to the ILO, in 2012 there will be 202 million people unemployed in the world, up 6 million from 2011.

Economic Growth Is the Key

To sum up the situation, in the United States increasing revenue is the key to managing the deficit. The more revenue, the more taxes will be collected. The economy needs to grow to finance the deficit. And the fact that much of Europe is in a recession and China also is slowing is bad news for the United States because of our trade links with them. Earnings have been stagnant— U.S. businesses have been negatively impacted from the effects of Europe's turmoil and China's slowdown. There is serious spillover from the troubled European banking system, stock market, and trade and consumer confidence here at home.

While the U.S. economy is growing and was technically pulled out of recession in 2009, we still need more economic growth and a higher tax base to fight the continuing deficit and debt. The economy in the United States is stagnant, and needs to be recharged. Our country had a fairly positive GDP uptick at 1.3 in 2010 and 2.1 in 2011. In the first quarter of 2012, GDP rose to 2.0 and the second estimate for the second quarter is 1.7. But remember—the economic health of the European nations and China is closely tied to the prosperity of the United States One fallen domino over there could quickly topple the wobbling U.S. economy.

In the next chapter we will examine the budget effects of U.S. fiscal policy. It's a cautionary tale, as the percentage of debt held by the public is rising compared to the economy's annual production. This is called the debt-to-GDP ratio, a rough indicator of the country's productive strength to handle the debt repayment. We will examine projections by leading economic agencies concerning the deficit, debt, and the debt-to-GDP ratio.

---

[6]International Labour Organization. *2012 World of Work Report: Summary.* Available at www.ilo.org (accessed July 27, 2012).

Deficit and Debt Projections

There are two ways to influence the economy—through fiscal policy (using government spending or taxation to impact the economy) or through monetary policy (adjusting money supply and interest rates to impact the economy). Some policy makers favor the deliberate actions of fiscal policies, others prefer the flexibility of monetary actions, while many advocate a powerful combination of the tools. All concur that unlike monetary policy, fiscal stimulus actions spur deficits. So let's take a quick look at how fiscal and monetary policy tools work. Then you can decide if the benefits of fiscal policies are worth such high deficits.

Fiscal and Monetary Policy

Leave the economy alone and it will correct itself. This was the laissez-faire policy advocated by the classical school of economic theory prior to the arrival of British economist John Maynard Keynes. After World War I, Keynes became a famous advocate of using fiscal policy to thrust a country's economy out of depression. Leaving the economy alone might eventually cause it to correct itself, but most Americans want a quicker response and are unwilling to wait for the economy to bloom on its own. Enter fiscal policy.

As mentioned, in macroeconomics there are two main policy tools used to influence the economy:

- *Monetary policy:* Manipulating the money supply and interest rates to influence the economy

- *Fiscal policy:* Adjusting government spending and/or taxation to achieve full employment, economic growth, and price stability

There's a huge debate within the economics community: monetary policy or fiscal policy—which will be quicker and more powerful to recharge the economy? Which strategy works best is a matter of debate among economists, politicians, and the public. In the United States, the Federal Reserve—the central bank of the United States—is in charge of monetary policy. Monetary policy is the process of managing the nation's money supply to influence the economy. The growth rate of money, in turn, affects the cost of money and the availability of credit. Fiscal policy is initiated by the president and Congress. Each year the president proposes to Congress a budget and tax changes for the upcoming fiscal year. This is a blueprint, or a starting point, for negotiations with Congress. The president can then accept or veto specific acts that Congress has passed.

Since before the onset of the recession in December 2007, the Federal Reserve ("the Fed"), with Ben Bernanke at the helm, has been pursuing an aggressive expansionary monetary policy to push short-term interest rates to low levels and keep the economy healthy. In addition, the Fed has bought mortgage-backed securities, Treasury securities, and government agency securities in an effort to push long-term rates down and stabilize asset prices. Monetary policy can fight inflation, economic slumps, and unemployment without incurring deficits.

Operating on the fiscal-policy side in 2009, the Obama administration ran a massive stimulus package aimed at jumpstarting the economy. It included tax cuts and large public works programs designed to create jobs and improve the infrastructure. For stimulating the economy or to move an economy out of a recession, some might argue that fiscal policy tends to be a winner in restoring output.

A *contractionary* fiscal policy is designed to suppress inflation during a rising boom period. To dampen demand for goods and services, the government decreases government expenditures and/or increases taxes. Monetary policy also can be used to dampen the economy. Hiking interest rates, for example, can slow an overcharged economy.

As a compromise, most policy analysts believe that some combination of fiscal and monetary policy is needed. The Fed's main tool of monetary policy is open market operations, the buying and selling of government bonds to expand or contract money supply. The key advantages of monetary policy are its flexibility and timeliness. Monetary policy is conducted at the direction of the Fed and can be implemented quickly, whereas the implementation of fiscal policy often faces political obstacles that slow it down. The impact of fiscal policy cannot be predicted with total accuracy, but when used appropriately, the effect on the real economy is direct and can influence the broad direction of the economy. Even Fed Chairman Bernanke recognizes the importance of using both tools. In his conclusion to a 2009 speech at the London School of Economics, Bernanke noted, "In the near term, the highest priority is to promote a global economic recovery. The Federal Reserve retains powerful policy tools and will use them aggressively to help achieve this objective. Fiscal policy can stimulate economic activity, but a sustained recovery will also require a comprehensive plan to stabilize the financial system and restore normal flows of credit."[1]

Macroeconomic Goals of Fiscal Policy

As previously stated, fiscal policy is the deliberate use of government spending and/or taxation to influence the overall level of economic activity. Because fiscal policy involves altering government spending or taxes, both of which impact the federal budget, it is linked directly to deficits and the national debt. Let's leave monetary policy behind now and concentrate on fiscal policy because of its connection to the deficit. One of the effects of utilizing fiscal policy is that the government may have difficulty balancing the budget and stimulating the economy simultaneously. In most cases, the government will run a deficit, which causes a rise in the national debt.

John Maynard Keynes (1883–1946), famous British economist and author of *The General Theory of Employment, Interest and Money* (1936), is known as the father of modern macroeconomics. The predominant theory at the time of the Great Depression, known as the classical theory, posits that the economy will eventually correct itself. It advocates a laissez-faire policy. Keynes disputed that theory and became well-known for promoting active fiscal policy to pull the United States out of recession. An advisor to President Franklin D. Roosevelt, Keynes encouraged the U.S. government to spend—and spend big. And indeed the government did, developing a host of programs in the 1930s and 1940s: Social Security, Income Security, and New Deal programs designed to encourage spending and overall business activity. Keynes felt the free market would not be powerful enough to increase aggregate demand during a downturn. He said it was the government's responsibility to stimulate aggregate demand.

---

[1]Ben S. Bernanke. "The Crisis and the Policy Response," speech delivered at the Stamp Lecture, London School of Economics, January 13, 2009. Available at www.federalreserve.gov/newsevents/speech/bernanke20090113a.htm.

Aggregate demand is the sum of all demand in an economy at a given time and price level. Aggregate demand, or gross domestic product (GDP), can be calculated by adding spending on consumer goods and services, investments by businesses, government spending, and net exports (total exports minus total imports). GDP measures the total level of demand for goods and services by all category groups within an economy. When total demand equals the level of total spending, the economy is in an equilibrium level. Using a simple model, let's assume that net exports are zero. Therefore, we have consumer, government, and business spending determining the equilibrium level of GDP. Fiscal policy is mainly employed by shifting aggregate demand. The government does this by changing spending or taxation, or a combination of both.

The Employment Act of 1946 charged the federal government with the responsibility of promoting a high level of employment, output, and purchasing power. These goals were restated in wider detail in the Full Employment and Balanced Growth Act of 1978, designed to "promote full employment, production, and real income, balanced growth, adequate productivity growth, proper attention to national priorities, and reasonable price stability."[2] Both acts support the government's use of fiscal policy to manage the U.S. economy.

Tools of Fiscal Policy

Fiscal policy can be implemented through two major means, adjusting taxes and/or making government purchases. There is a third policy option, using both tools at the same time. It is a detailed process that can have a powerful impact on the economy.

Taxes

Income taxes are paid as a percentage of income. So, the level of spending by individuals and businesses is affected by tax rates. People base their spending on after-tax income, or disposable income. Businesses base their discretionary spending and investment decisions on after-tax profits.

If the economy is booming and experiencing inflation, Congress might increase taxes. This would result in a reduction in aggregate demand because it reduces both consumer spending and business investment. Therefore, a higher tax rate reduces business activity and consequently dampens inflation. Conversely, by lowering the tax rate for consumers and businesses, disposable income and profits will be higher, stimulating the economy and helping to reduce unemployment. This fiscal policy would increase aggregate demand.

---

[2]Full Employment and Balanced Growth Act of 1978, 15 USC § 3101 (1978); excerpt from the Bill Summary.

As a fiscal tool, tax cuts have less impact on aggregate demand than government spending of the same size. The reason? Each dollar of government spending goes directly into the economy to stimulate GDP. But with a tax cut, only a portion will be spent by individuals and businesses; the rest will be saved.

A tax credit is another type of tax incentive that can be used to shift aggregate demand. An investment tax credit, for example, allows a business to use a portion of the price of new capital equipment as a credit to reduce its tax liability. Congress might raise the investment tax credit to get the economy out of a rut or to revitalize employment. Businesses would be incentivized to spend more on investment capital, thereby stimulating business activity and raising aggregate demand. To help reduce inflation, Congress can decrease the investment tax credit, which restricts business activity and lowers aggregate demand.

Government Spending

The government can influence aggregate demand either by buying more goods and services or by decreasing purchases. If the economy is booming and inflation is a problem, Congress might decrease government spending to lower aggregate demand. Slower overall business activity dampens inflation. On the other hand, the simplest way to raise aggregate demand is to increase government spending because the funds flow directly into the economy. If unemployment is high, Congress might increase government spending to raise aggregate demand.

The Multiplier Effect

The *multiplier effect* is the idea that spending a dollar, or cutting taxes a dollar, will result in even greater returns to the economy. Estimations of multipliers attempt to calculate the cumulative effects of fiscal policy actions, such as a reduction in taxes or an increase in government spending. When the government spends money, that spending translates into income for individuals and businesses, who then re-spend that money. The cycle of spending results in a cumulative impact of the initial amount on total economic activity.

Tax multipliers are smaller than government spending multipliers because a tax cut is not a direct infusion into the economy. A tax cut increases disposable income, which then increases consumption. Let's look at the simple government spending multiplier to get a feel for how the process works. Every dollar of income is either consumed or saved. The marginal propensity to consume (MPC) is the fraction of additional income that households will consume versus save (MPS). If the MPC is 0.8 then the MPS is 0.2.

The government spending multiplier is 1/MPS or 1/1 − MPC. Assume a $100 million increase in government spending and an MPC of 0.8. The spending multiplier of 1/1 − MPC equates to 1/1 − 0.8, or a spending multiplier of 5. Government spending will result in a rise of output by $500 million (5 × $100 million). The larger the MPC, the more powerful the multiplier impact.

Estimates of current-day fiscal multipliers vary widely, but tend to fall under 3. As an example, the Congressional Budget Office (CBO), an investigative economic arm of the U.S. government, has utilized macroeconomic forecasting models to estimate the impact of the recent Obama stimulus package (American Recovery and Reinvestment Act of 2009[3]). According to the CBO, a one-time $1 increase in the purchase of goods and services can produce up to $1 to $2.50 of new economic activity. Tax cuts are not as stimulative as government spending, according to the CBO. For $1 of 2-year tax cuts for lower- and middle-income households, output can rise between $0.60 and $1.50. For $1 of 1-year tax cuts for higher-income households, output can rise between $0.20 and $0.60.

Discretionary Fiscal Policy

Discretionary fiscal policy is a fiscal policy that is acted on by Congress in response to economic conditions. Discretionary fiscal policy may be contractionary or expansionary. Discretionary fiscal policy is an attempt to influence the overall economy toward high employment and price stability. These actions will move the economy in a more expedited manner than would be possible if it were left alone.

Contractionary fiscal policy involves decreasing government purchases or increasing taxes. If policymakers have concerns about rising inflation, they could use contractionary fiscal policy to reduce increasing aggregate demand. If people and businesses are spending too freely and price and wage increases start to spiral upward, Congress could attempt to dampen spending. When the government spends less, fewer funds are available in the economy to purchase goods and services. Raising taxes also reduces the amount of money in the hands of both consumers and businesses. The resulting decreased spending will slow the price and wage spiral.

Expansionary fiscal policy involves an increase in government spending or a decrease in taxes. This would be used to raise aggregate demand, thereby boosting employment, but it may also cause some inflation. When the

---

[3]Congressional Budget Office. *Estimated Impact of the American Recovery and Reinvestment Act on Employment and Economic Output from October 2010 Through December 2010,* February 2011. Available at www.cbo.gov (accessed February 27, 2011).

government spends, more money is pumped into the economy and people have more funds to buy clothes, computers, cars, and food. Businesses will have more money for investment and production. Reducing taxes also puts more money in the hands of consumers and businesses. It can have an inflationary aspect to it if spending erupts.

Table 4-1 summarizes the impact of both contractionary and expansionary policies.

Table 4-1. Discretionary Fiscal Policy Stance

Type of Policy	Picture of the Economy	Taxes	Government Spending
Contractionary	Booming and inflation	Raised	Lowered
Expansionary	Slowdown or recession	Lowered	Raised

The Supply Siders

Increasing or decreasing aggregate demand is the mainstay of fiscal policy strategies. Nevertheless, there is an alternative economic theory that puts the emphasis on supply. Supply side economics focuses on increasing the supply of goods and services. It had its heyday during the time of Ronald Reagan's presidency.

Economist Arthur Laffer (1940–) was a member of President Ronald Reagan's Economic Policy Advisory Board from 1981 to 1989. Laffer promoted tax cuts to businesses and individuals to stimulate investment. The supply side theory posits that this will increase employment and long-term economic growth. The marginal tax rate is the rate of taxes paid on the last dollar earned, and "Laffer's curve" supported the notion that if the marginal tax rates were cut, output would rise. Why? Because firms would invest more capital in their businesses and workers would provide more labor. Supply siders maintain that as the supply of goods and services rises, prices fall. The lower prices encourage people to purchase. The increased output in society generates larger tax revenue and thus decreases the budget deficit.

Laffer, commonly referred to as the father of supply side economics, won many followers by advocating that a tax cut can increase tax revenue. Sound too good to be true? Perhaps. It was tested during the Reagan era; taxes were cut deeply during his time in office, and the deficit and national debt rose significantly. However, another problem contributed to the situation—the plan was not fully implemented, as the tax cuts were accompanied by increased government spending. Today, it is widely recognized that tax cuts without spending cuts would increase the budget deficit. Although not a mainstream economic fiscal policy, supply side economic policy continues to stir discussion in the profession.

Transfer Payments

Some fiscal policy is automatic. Automatic fiscal policy does not require a vote by Congress. Transfer payments are government payments for which no current productive service or product is exchanged. These include Social Security, welfare, and unemployment. Here's how it works. When the economy is in a recession, many people are not working—unemployment is high. But the government automatically provides unemployment insurance to more people and provides them additional disposable income to spend. Those people then have funds to buy groceries, gasoline, clothing, and so forth, and the economy is automatically recharged. So transfer payments can help keep aggregate demand from falling precipitously. When the economy enters a prosperous period, there's an automatic reduction in transfers, and thus a decrease in money coming into the economy. Remember that this form of automatic fiscal policy is not a direct dollar injection into spending because consumers still have the choice to save a percentage of their transfer payments.

Progressive Income Taxes

The federal government's tax system is progressive. That means the tax rate increases as income increases. The tax system is an automatic stabilizer, meaning it will smooth out fluctuations in aggregate demand automatically. No act of Congress is required. In an expansionary period, greater economic activity means individuals and businesses whose income increases are thrown into a higher tax bracket. Consequently, a greater percentage of income must go to paying taxes. This slows the growth of spending, dampening aggregate demand and relieving inflationary concerns. For consumers and businesses, when income rises during an expansionary period, being pushed into a higher tax bracket is akin to withdrawing a bit of money out of one's piggy bank. The flip scenario occurs when a recession appears. Incomes are reduced, and people and businesses fall into lower tax brackets. They pay a lower marginal tax rate and contribute less to the government's tax revenue. This is akin to an automatic tax cut, which provides more purchasing power to stimulate aggregate demand. For consumers and businesses, when incomes are reduced during a recessionary period, being pushed into a lower tax bracket is akin to putting a bit of money back in the piggy bank.

Criticism of Discretionary Fiscal Policy

There are definitely some problems associated with implementing fiscal policy. The old adage "easier said than done" certainly applies to the various fiscal policy tools. Before we examine current and historical examples of fiscal policy, let's look at some of the drawbacks of using fiscal tools. It will be a helpful background when evaluating real-life fiscal policies. Specifically, there are four concerns that are of note: time lags, the political process, human behavior, and crowding out.

Time Lags

The first issue is that the government must recognize the fact an economic problem has developed. By relying on economic data for validation, many months may pass before the president and Congress identify a problem. Then time must be allocated to developing taxation and government spending policies to address the issue. Devising economic policies takes time, and funding for such actions needs to be added to the next year's budget. Central to all this is Congress's approval of the budget. If it is a government spending package, it will take time for the money to be spent and multiply throughout the economy. If the solution is a tax cut, it may take a very long time for spending to actually increase from consumers' extra disposable income. And then, to top it off, the overall picture of the economy could shift again, even while the policy is being implemented, and the action could actually have a negative counter effect on the nation's economy.

Political Process

Fiscal policy involves the adjustment of government spending and/or tax levels and is controlled by the politicians in Congress. And let's face it—it is never popular when politicians increase taxes and reduce government spending. Furthermore, because politicians are beholden to the constituents in their respective state or district, they are unlikely to willingly eliminate projects that benefit those constituents. Even though a particular fiscal policy might be the best action for the United States as a whole, some of the decisions may not be well received by individuals and businesses. Politicians are elected officials, and it is a reality that many are swayed by the vote.

Human Behavior

There is a great deal of psychology connected to implementing fiscal policy. Fiscal policy relies on accurately predicting how people will react, and there are no guarantees in how people will behave. For example, a tax cut may be made under the assumption that people and businesses will get out and spend, thus stimulating aggregate demand. In reality, consumers have a choice. They may spend a significant portion of the increase in their disposable income, as expected, resulting in an uptick in output. Or they may actually save the additional funds or pay down debt. Just because consumers reacted a particular way in the past does not mean that they will always follow the same direction, as economic conditions shift.

Crowding Out

As mentioned, when the government cuts taxes and/or increases government spending, this is referred to as an expansionary fiscal policy. Expansionary fiscal policy is financed by deficit spending. A detrimental effect is that interest rates will rise as the government competes for funds to finance its deficit. In turn, this makes it more difficult for the private sector to borrow money, and thus expansion by the private sector segment is dampened.

History of Fiscal Policies

Looking at U.S. history, we can see that some fiscal policies have been highly successful, while others have been partially successful or even unsuccessful. Let's look at some of the more notable fiscal events in history. You will see the difficulty of predicting not only the ultimate result of these polices, but also if consumers will behave as anticipated.

Great Depression

Fiscal policy came to be used as an economic tool during the Great Depression era. To get a picture of just how devastating the Depression era was, check out some economic facts. In October 1929, the stock market plummeted 23 percent during a 2-day period, the result of rampant specu-lation and buying stocks on margin. Yet the stock market crash was just a symptom of the Depression. There were many causes, such as a contrac-tion of the money supply and widespread banking failures, that led to the decline in the U.S. economy. The collapse began in the United States but quickly turned into a worldwide economic contraction. The downturn was particularly significant in the United States, lasting for over a decade across the country.

Another driving factor was a momentous drop in spending—aggregate demand—leading the country's business production to be cut in half. At the height of the Depression, one-third of the nonfarm workforce was unem-ployed and one-fourth of all workers were unemployed. The human suffering and devastation was significant, and among the catastrophic statistics, the suicide rate rose considerably during that time period.

During the 1930s, it was the federal government that acted, using fiscal tools, to influence the level of aggregate demand. When Franklin D. Roosevelt (FDR) stepped into the presidency in 1933, he enacted a variety of programs to stim-ulate the economy, give jobs to people, and initiate reforms so that such wide-spread poverty and devastation would not occur again. Much of what FDR initiated was based on the advice of John Maynard Keynes, using Keynesian fiscal tools to promote economic growth. Their goal was to put money in the people's hands through the various programs. They believed government spending would stimulate the economy.

The New Deal work programs, such as the Work Projects Administration (WPA), put unemployed people to work again (Figure 4-1) building schools, roads, bridges, and other community projects in most communities across the United States. FDR's policy succeeded in employing millions of workers, enabling them to spend and stimulate the economy. The programs were widespread—welfare programs, Social Security, banking reforms (including deposit insurance), and New Deal Work programs were all used to revive the economy.

Figure 4-1. In this January 1939 photograph, a Work Projects Administration (WPA) employee receives his paycheck at a construction site. The WPA was the largest and best known of the New Deal programs created to employ Americans during the Great Depression. At the end of the project, $11 billion had been spent, with 8 million workers completing a variety of public projects including parks, schools, roads, and bridges. *Source: The National Archives, Records of the Works Project Administration.*

FDR was cautious not to run large deficits during his tenure. His deficits were modest, and in 1937 he actually had a balanced budget. In reality, he did not fully utilize deficit spending to cure the Great Depression economy. Consequently, it was not until the huge spending increases at the beginning of World War II, in 1941, that the economy did finally recover fully.

World War II

The government incurred massive deficit spending in the effort to finance World War II. The conclusion of most economists is that it was the government's spending for WWII that finally ended the Great Depression. According to the Bureau of the Public Debt, government expenditures during WWII were roughly $323 billion, and approximately $211 billion of this total was borrowed money.[4] The U.S. Treasury Department got in gear to help fund this massive spending spree, creating a new security instrument—the nonmarketable small-denomination Savings Bond. The average worker could afford this security, and purchasing War Bonds, as they were called, became a patriotic obligation. Deficit spending had put an end to the most severe depression in history, and fiscal policy would now be an active tool utilized by the government to restore the economy.

Kennedy-Johnson Tax Cut

An "A" grade goes to the Kennedy–Johnson tax cuts, which were right on track in stimulating the economy and largely praised as a successful fiscal plan. Historic income tax reductions of $11.5 billion on personal and corporate taxes were enacted over a 2-year period in 1964 and 1965. President Kennedy's platform was that the country was not at maximum income and employment levels, and that economic growth should increase at the rate of 4 percent each year. Kennedy's fiscal plan spelled out the use of deficit spending to stimulate economic activity, and it did bring the predicted result of spurring on a sluggish U.S. economy. It wasn't until after Kennedy's death that President Johnson signed the historic tax reduction bill, in February 1964. Johnson aptly used his persuasive skills, asking Americans to spend the increase in their incomes from the tax reduction.

Economic Stimulus Act of 2008

In 2008, President George W. Bush signed a $168 billion economic stimulus package. It reduced federal revenue by $152 billion in fiscal year 2008, followed

---

[4]Bureau of the Public Debt. "Our History." Available at
www.publicdebt.treas.gov/history/history.htm (accessed February 6, 2011).

by $16 billion in fiscal 2009. The intent was to minimize the effects of the recessionary downturn precipitated by the worldwide financial crisis that began in 2007. The package included tax breaks to businesses for equipment purchases, and widely touted tax rebates to individual taxpayers. Most people received a $600 tax rebate check, and married couples received $1,200. Taxpayers were encouraged to spend their stimulus money to revive the economy, and consumer spending was expected to recharge the economy. Although low levels of aggregate demand may have increased, the overwhelming conclusion is that the stimulus package did not work. The stimulus checks ran up the budget deficit and taxpayers did not spend as anticipated. Instead, the biggest share of Americans used their money to pay down debt or put it into savings.

American Recovery and Reinvestment Act of 2009

President Barack Obama signed the $787 billion American Recovery and Reinvestment Act (ARRA) in 2009, designed to boost economic activity and employment. Its premise was to thwart the recession by creating jobs and increasing investment and consumer expenditures. Tax cuts and spending programs, including for local governments, energy, health care, infrastructure, science, and education, were targeted to boost economic progress. How is it working? Overwhelming evidence suggests the fiscal package may have had modest effects. The judge and jury are still out, but some recent findings by the CBO suggest the effects are waning.

A recent report released by the CBO during the fourth quarter of 2010 reveals some interesting findings.[5] First of all, the study suggests the cost of the recovery package during the fiscal years 2009 to 2019 period will amount to a whopping $821 billion. Almost half of this budgetary impact is reported to have occurred in fiscal year 2010. The number is on the rise, as this is $7 billion more than anticipated in the previous quarterly report. The ARRA was passed in February 2009, and as of the fourth quarter of 2009 it was estimated that the bill had the effect of increasing the number of employed people by between 900,000 and 1.9 million. A year later, in the fourth quarter of 2010, the range had widened to between 1.3 and 3.5 million people. ARRA's policies impacted fourth quarter 2010 by raising real GDP between 1.1 and 3.5 percent, and lowered the unemployment rate between 0.7 and 1.9 percentage points.

---

[5]Congressional Budget Office. *Estimated Impact of the American Recovery and Reinvestment Act on Employment and Economic Output from October 2010 Through December 2010.* February 2011. Available at www.cbo.gov (Accessed February 27, 2011).

But, according to the CBO report, the effects of the ARRA on output peaked in the first half of 2010 and are now retreating, as would be expected. Employment and unemployment are forecast to lag slightly behind the effect on output, or GDP, but that too is anticipated to fall in 2011. The effect of the ARRA policies is estimated to raise real GDP modestly in 2011, between 0.7 and 2.2 percent. The unemployment rate will be lowered between 0.5 and 1.4 percentage points. Perhaps most notable is the estimate for future economic activity, as reported in the Director's Blog of the CBO: "During 2012, the CBO estimates that the impact on employment and economic output of ARRA will be small."[6]

A recent update on the projected effects of ARRA for 2012, shows that the stimulus package will increase deficits $833 billion over the 2009–2019 period, with more than 90 percent of the budgetary impact occurring by June 2012. The CBO notes that the effects are diminishing, projecting an impact on real GDP at between 0.1 and 0.8 for 2012, along with increase the number of employed between 0.2 to 1.2 million. Despite some modest near-term benefits, according to the CBO, "ARRA will actually reduce output slightly in the long run, CBO estimates—by between zero and 0.2 percent after 2016." In addition, the CBO estimates that the act will have no long-term effects on employment because of a high rate of use of its labor resources in the long run.[7]

Debt-to-GDP Ratio

Table 4-2 shows federal government debt as a percentage of GDP. It compares gross federal debt and net federal debt (the debt held by the public, less the portion of debt internally held by the government) to GDP. GDP tells the story of the output of the country. Specifically, it is the market value of all final goods and services produced in the economy for a specific time period, namely a year. Both are good indicators of a nation's productive ability to handle its debt repayment.

As Table 4-2 projected, gross federal debt did top 100 percent of the nation's productive capacity in 2012. Roughly, this suggests it would take the country the entire value of output—everyone working for a full year—to cover its debt level.

---

[6]Benjamin Page and Felix Reichling, CBO Macroeconomic Analysis Division, "Estimated Impact of ARRA on Employment and Economic Output from October 2010 through December 2010," Congressional Budget Office Director's Blog, February 23, 2011. http://cboblog.cbo.gov/?p=1852 (accessed February 24, 2011).
[7]Congressional Budget Office. *Estimated Impact of the American Recovery and Reinvestment Act on Employment and Economic Output from April 2012 Through June 2012*, August 2012. Available at www.cbo.gov (accessed September 12, 2012), p. 8.

Table 4-2. Federal Debt As a Percentage of GDP

	Gross Federal Debt	Net Federal Debt
1940	52.4 %	44.2 %
1950	94.1 %	80.2 %
1960	56.0 %	45.6 %
1970	37.6 %	28.0 %
1980	33.4 %	26.1 %
1990	55.9 %	42.1 %
2000	57.3 %	34.7 %
2010	94.2 %	62.8 %
2011	98.7 %	67.7 %
2012 (estimate)	104.8 %	74.2 %
2013 (estimate)	107.4 %	77.4 %
2014 (estimate)	107.8 %	78.4 %
2015 (estimate)	106.9 %	78.1 %
2016 (estimate)	105.9 %	77.8 %
2017 (estimate)	104.7 %	77.1 %

Source: Budget of the U.S. Government, FY 2013 Historical Tables, Table 7.1, "Federal Debt at the End of Year: 1940–2017."

Table 4-2 also shows that the debt, both gross and net, is rising in size relative to GDP. This is a sign that the national debt is expanding in relation to its productive strength. It was in 1946, after WWII, that the debt reached an alarming all-time high of 121.7 percent gross debt to GDP, and 108.7 percent net debt to GDP. Other notable periods that pushed the debt-to-GDP numbers high include the huge tax cuts during the Reagan administration (1981–1989), which set the debt on a path of nearly tripling, and the 2007 recession, which caused tax revenue to drop, with federal spending reaching an all-time high.

U.S. Record Debt

Economists view the net federal debt, relative to GDP, as the most telling indicator of economic stability—or economic woe—when it comes to the debt level. At the end of 2000, the amount of net federal debt stood at nearly 35 percent of the economy's production, but has now risen to over 70 percent. The 10-year rise starting in 2000, as the debt nearly doubled in size, pushed the debt-to-GDP numbers upward. The CBO predicts a continuing upward trend, culminating in the high 70 percent range by 2017. And according to the CBO, net federal debt is expected to rise to 87 percent of GDP by 2020. Worst-case scenario analysis by the CBO predicts the United States will owe 854 percent of GDP by 2080. Although it is perhaps not likely the U.S. economy will climb into staggering numbers such as this, it is a definite possibility.

What is the proper level of debt to GDP? That is a matter of debate among economists. Look around. For 2011, comparisons range widely, from 163.343 percent for Greece and 80.432 percent for France, to New Zealand at 8.308 percent and Denmark at 2.636213 percent. Although there is no uniform standard, virtually all professional economists comment on the startling upward climb of the debt-to-GDP ratio for the United States. In a July 2010 International Monetary Fund (IMF) *Selected Issues* paper discussing the financing of U.S. deficits, it is noted, "Under current policies, the United States federal debt is projected to grow rapidly due to a combination of large budget deficits before and during the crisis, as well as, over the medium term, demographic factors and healthcare inflation." The recommendations provided by the IMF, which monitors government debt levels, conclude, "As part of the medium term adjustment, the authorities would need to raise taxes and/or cut transfers substantially to avoid an undesirable escalation of the debt-to-GDP ratio."[8]

Any way you report it, the U.S. deficit is huge. The Office of Management and Budget (OMB), which is the executive agency division of the Executive Office of the President, prepares and administers the federal budget, and forms projections for the debt for upcoming years. Take a look at Table 4-3. Deficit projections for fiscal year 2012 stand at over $1.3 trillion, falling to the $600 billion range beginning in fiscal year 2014. Estimates for the deficit as a percentage of GDP hit 8.5 percent for 2012, falling gradually to 3.0 percent as of 2017. The debt, which closed fiscal year 2011 at roughly $14.8 trillion, is projected to hit over $21 trillion by 2017, according to the OMB numbers. Gross debt as a percentage of GDP stood at 98.7 percent in 2011, with estimates showing a slow rise to 107.4 percent by 2014, before declining. These are staggering accounts of a country facing budgetary challenges.

Table 4-3. Debt and Deficit Projections by the Office of Management and Budget (in millions of dollars)

	Gross Federal Debt	Deficit
2010	$13,528,807	$1,293,489
2011	$14,764,222	$1,299,595
2012 (estimate)	$16,350,885	$1,326,948
2013 (estimate)	$17,547,936	$901,408
2014 (estimate)	$18,499,909	$667,802
2015 (estimate)	$19,426,503	$609,713
2016 (estimate)	$20,391,198	$648,755
2017 (estimate)	$21,325,493	$612,448

Source: Budget of the U.S. Government, FY 2013 Historical Tables, Table 7.1, "Federal Debt at the End of Year: 1940–2016," and Table 1.1, "Summary of Receipts, Outlays, and Surpluses or Deficits: 1789–2017.

---

[8]International Monetary Fund. United States: Selected Issues Paper, "IMF Country Report No. 10/248," July 2010. Washington, D.C. Available at www.imf.org (accessed February 27, 2011), p. 56.

Of particular interest, the CBO notes in its report that the economy has struggled to pull out of the recession, and recovery is slow since the recession ended in June 2009. There have been sharply lower revenues, topped with increased spending, from the financial turmoil and a drop in output. The CBO also mentions the aging U.S. population and paying for the rising costs of health care. These factors will likely push the federal government spending-as-a-percentage-of-GDP figure well above that of recent decades.

The unemployment rate is expected to fall, but it is a gradual process, shifting from 8.8 in 2011, to 5.3 percent in 2022. The CBO projects the economy will be impacted by the lingering effects of the recession and financial crisis over the next 2 years but anticipates real GDP to pick up to a modest 4.1 percent in the years 2014 to 2017. Although high by historical measures the deficit is projected to start shrinking within the next few years. The level of decrease is dependent on the overall recovery of the economy and policymakers actions related to taxation and spending policies that are scheduled to take effect in 2013 under current law.

The Congressional Budget Office released its annual *Budget and Economic Outlook* for fiscal years 2012 to 2022. As shown in Table 4-4, assuming current law remains unchanged, the CBO predicts the federal deficit will dip below $1 trillion beginning in fiscal 2013, and debt held by the public will rise to over $15 trillion in fiscal 2022.

Table 4-4. Congressional Budget Office Baseline Budget Outlook (in billions of dollars)

	Debt Held by Public	Deficit
2011 (actual)	$10,128	$1,296
2012	$11,242	$1,079
2013	$11,945	$585
2014	$12,401	$345
2015	$12,783	$269
2016	$13,188	$302
2017	$13,509	$220
2018	$13,801	$196
2019	$14,148	$258
2020	$14,512	$280
2021	$14,872	$279
2022	$15,291	$339

Source: Congressional Budget Office, The Budget and Economic Outlook: Fiscal Years 2012 to 2022, Summary Table 1, "CBO's Baseline Budget Outlook."

Summary

Monetary policy, at the direction of the Federal Reserve, involves regulating money supply and interest rates. Strengths of monetary policy include its flexibility and ability to be implemented quickly. To achieve the best results for the economy, many policymakers advocate using both monetary and fiscal policies. Through fiscal policy, a deliberate act to influence the economy, the deficit can rise. Fiscal policy is a powerful tool that the president and Congress can use to affect output and minimize inflation. Automatic stabilizers, too, can affect the deficit situation.

Federal debt to GDP is a good indicator of a nation's productive ability to pay back its debt. At the end of 2012, gross federal debt to GDP stood at 103 percent. The projected trend for debt to GDP is upward. This is a negative sign that the debt is expanding in comparison to its productive ability.

Should you be worried about the rising debt? Why are there so many grassroots groups monitoring our country's deficit and debt levels? Read on. In the next chapter we'll ponder this crucial question: Do deficits and the debt matter?

Do Deficits and the Debt Matter?

The deficit debate has been brewing for decades. Notably, it was the thirty-second U.S. president, Franklin D. Roosevelt, who was against hiking deficits. FDR was a four-term president (1933–1945), elected in November 1932, in the midst of the devastating Great Depression. During his presidency, FDR instituted Social Security, welfare reforms, new banking controls, and New Deal programs. FDR did incur modest deficits in an attempt to restore the economy and assist the unemployed. However, "FDR refused to run up the deficits that ending the depression required," according to the Eleanor Roosevelt Papers. Early efforts did bring recovery to output, but "only when the federal government imposed rationing, recruited 6 million defense workers (including women and African-Americans), drafted 6 million soldiers, and ran massive deficits to fight World War II, did the Great Depression finally end."[1]

Recent Deficit Issues

Let's fast-forward to the twenty-first century, when the deficit issue has once again taken center stage. According to Pulitzer Prize winner Ron Suskind's book, *The Price of Loyalty*, a notable event occurred in late 2002, at a meeting of President George W. Bush's economic team. During the meeting, with

---

[1]The Eleanor Roosevelt Papers. "The Great Depression," *Teaching Eleanor Roosevelt*, edited by Allida Black, June Hopkins, et al. (Hyde Park, NY: Eleanor Roosevelt National Historic Site, 2003). Available at www.gwu.edu/~erpapers/teachinger/glossary/great-depression.cfm (accessed September 15, 2012).

the theme "economic growth," Vice President Dick Cheney chatted with the White House staff and the economic team. Cheney mentioned that cutting the tax on dividends for individuals would provide some stimulating effects to the economy. Treasury Secretary Paul H. O'Neill, concerned that the country didn't need a second round of tax cuts, argued that the government "is moving toward a fiscal crisis." Cheney retorted, "Reagan proved that deficits don't matter."[2] O'Neill was shocked by Cheney's comment because he was concerned about what a tax cut would do to the rising deficits. To O'Neill, deficits clearly mattered. The following month, Cheney called O'Neill, told him the president wanted a new team on board, and fired him.

While the deficit in 2002 was relatively low, $158 billion, compared to more recent deficits, many politicians and economists have agreed for years with the sentiment expressed by Dick Cheney that deficits are not a major concern. There is a faction of economists and politicians that still holds this view. But with the United States running trillion-dollar deficits for four straight years, the political argument has now shifted. The trend of late is to profess that "deficits do matter."

Changing Demographics

The U.S. population demographic is one area in which everyone is in agreement. We are an aging society. According to the U.S. Census Bureau, today 13 percent of the population is 65 years old and older. But in 2030, when all of the Baby Boomers will have reached retirement age, almost 20 percent of the population is projected to be 65 and older. The United States needs to focus now on how we are going to care for the elderly in future years and fund the already-stressed entitlement programs for the aged, such as Social Security and Medicaid.

These entitlement programs for retirees have traditionally been paid by the taxes of current workers—a pay-as-you-go system. But by 2030, the increase in retired workers brings the ratio of working age people down to 55 percent, to support the projected 20 percent of those 65 and over. That means a dramatic decline in the funds coming in to support our aging population. The current forecast is that the shifting demographics in the United States will likely place a major strain on the deficit and national debt, unless a solution can be found very soon.

Repercussions of Large Deficits

At some point in the future, with such large deficits, it's possible that citizens and foreign governments may lose confidence in the ability of the U.S. government to pay back holders of its debt instruments. Huge deficits, for example,

---

[2]Ron Suskind. *The Price of Loyalty* (New York: Simon & Schuster, 2004), p. 291.

are a red flag when it comes to issuing new debt. Traditionally, the Treasury has been able to sell debt with a low interest rate because its repayment is backed by the full faith and credit of the U.S. government. Treasuries are perceived to be risk-free. The United States has never defaulted, so most people believe that it will not default on the bonds that it sells.

But if citizens and other buyers of Treasury securities begin to think a default is possible, they will either demand exceptionally high interest rates or not invest in them at all. This would cause a snowball effect. If interest costs rise, interest payments will skyrocket, further stressing the budget. If concerns spread about the safety of government bonds, the government will be forced to offer higher, more attractive interest rates to buyers. It's a risk-return trade-off for investors. Again, if investors perceive government bonds to be more risky than other investments, they will demand a higher rate of return for the higher risk they are being exposed to.

With a loss of confidence, foreign investors may also reduce Treasury investments in a large way, which would be a disturbing trend because U.S. Treasuries have always been viewed as a safe haven worldwide. In addition, the U.S. dollar has always been the leader in global financial markets. The number one creditor, China, has already reduced its holdings significantly over the last year. The country held $1.307 trillion in Treasuries in June 2011 but dropped to just $1.164 trillion in June 2012. A large retreat would suggest that foreign investors lack confidence in the fiscal discipline of the largest economy. The effects of the loss of confidence may result in an unpredictable world-wide financial crisis. The United States is the world's economic leader and, with a GDP over $15 trillion, has the largest output in the world. That size makes the United States capable of helping to strengthen the world economic picture or sending a financial scare across the globe. A U.S. economy unable to attract securities buyers would have ramifications around the world. The United States would lose its financial, monetary, and political clout in the international arena.

Projected and Historical Trends of Debt

The historical graph shown in Figure 5-1 gives a quick overview of why concerns are growing about the U.S. debt. The graph shows an important fiscal measurement, debt held by the public (which excludes the amount of debt held by government trust funds and other government accounts) relative to GDP. The debt held by the public relative to output, or productive capacity, has taken a sharp turn upward over the past 10 years. The highest level, in 1946, was a product of World War II, and if many of the current policies are continued the second highest level will be reached by the end of 2022.

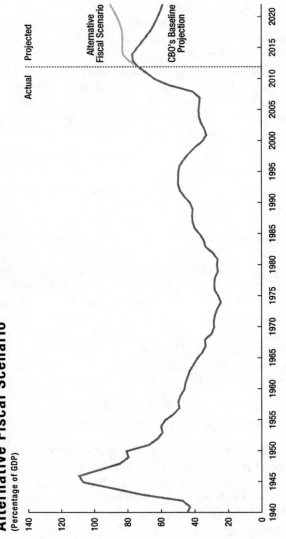

Federal Debt Held by the Public, Historically and As Projected in CBO's Baseline and Under an Alternative Fiscal Scenario

(Percentage of GDP)

August 2012
http://go.usa.gov/7QY

If current laws governing taxes and spending remain in effect (CBO's baseline projection), debt held by the public will fall from 73 percent of GDP in fiscal year 2012 to 58 percent of GDP in 2022. If policymakers altered those laws to maintain many policies that have been in effect in recent years (CBO's alternative fiscal scenario), debt would climb to 90 percent of GDP by 2022. In either case, debt would be relatively high by historical standards.

Figure 5-1. Federal debt held by the public as a percentage of GDP. *Source: Congressional Budget Office, The Budget and Economic Outlook: Fiscal Years 2012 to 2022, January 2012*

Along with historical trends, Figure 5-1 also shows two federal debt projections by the Congressional Budget Office (CBO). The extended-baseline scenario, sometimes called current law projections, adheres most closely to current laws of taxation and spending. These include the automatic enforcement of spending cuts and allowing tax cuts to expire. The alternative fiscal scenario shows the projection if many current laws and policies continued. According to recent update to The Budget and Economic Outlook (released August 22, 2012) the extended-baseline scenario paints a gloomy picture, showing that by 2022 the debt held by the public could equal roughly 58 percent of GDP, high by historical standards. The alternative fiscal scenario shows startling numbers, hitting a whopping 90 percent of GDP by 2022. Policymakers can have a huge impact on the debt path, and under the alternative fiscal scenario the debt would reach an unsustainable path and do significant harm to the economy.

Widespread Concern

The sentiments concerning the exploding deficits and rising debt are so strong; many national organizations have been formed that are dedicated to advocating generationally responsible fiscal policy. One prominent group is a nonpartisan organization founded in 1992 by the late former Senator Paul Tsongas (D-MA), former Senator Warren Rudman (R-NH), and former U.S. Secretary of Commerce Peter Peterson. The Concord Coalition, as it is called, is "dedicated to educating the public about the causes and consequences of federal budget deficits, the long-term challenges facing America's unsustainable entitlement programs, and how to build a sound economy for future generations."[3]

More evidence of the widespread deficit concerns mounting across the nation has been the outburst of unaffiliated groups called Tea Parties. The name comes from the Boston Tea Party in 1773, where colonists, objecting to a tax on tea levied by the British government, dumped 45 tons of tea into Boston Harbor. It was a protest not only against Britain, but also against the East India Company, which had been granted a monopoly on the importation of tea into the American colonies. In early 2009, as U.S. citizens became alarmed by what appeared to them as out-of-control government spending, self-organized groups began sprouting, using the Tea Party name as a basis for their political platform. These millions of concerned citizens, who believe in limited government, fiscal restraint, and lower taxes, hold Tea Party rallies to protest excessive government spending and the associated higher taxes required to finance such spending. The movement is a grassroots endeavor

---

[3]The Concord Coalition. "About the Concord Coalition." Available at www.concordcoalition.org/about-concord-coalition (accessed March 27, 2011).

with no specific leader. Without question, former Alaskan governor and 2008 Republican Vice Presidential candidate Sarah Palin is a favorite of the movement. Palin was the headline speaker at the first Tea Party Convention, held in Nashville, Tennessee in early 2010. How widespread is the political movement? In a *USA Today*/Gallup poll conducted in January 2011, results show 3 out of 10 Americans identify themselves as supporters of the Tea Party movement.[4]

A more recent poll, in April 2012, shows 41% support at least some of the Tea Party's goals.[5]

AN INTERVIEW WITH BILL FRENZEL

Bill Frenzel is well-versed on the federal debt and deficit issues. He was a U.S. Congressman for 20 years, and was the ranking minority member on the House Budget Committee. Frenzel served as a special advisor to President Bill Clinton on North America Free Trade Agreement (NAFTA), was appointed by President George W. Bush to the Social Security Commission in 2001 and in 2005, was appointed to Bush's Tax Reform Commission. He is cochairman of the Committee for a Responsible Federal Budget, cochairman of the Center for Strategic Tax Reform, and a guest scholar at the Brookings Institution. Frenzel frames some issues surrounding the debt debate.

   1.   *Is there a positive side to deficit spending?*

Yes. Deficit financing defends us in real emergencies. But running big deficits in "normal" times is what has put us in trouble.

   2.   *Has the U.S. ever found deficit spending useful in a crisis?*

Yes. That's how we got through most of our wars (WW II) and some of our recessions, and how we supported our financial system (TARP) when it was in crisis.

   3.   *How should we correct current U.S. fiscal woes?*

Technically, it's easy; politically it appears to be next to impossible. Just apply a Bowles-Simpson approach, phasing in a negotiated mixture of spending cuts and increased revenues, which stress reduction of the large, fast-rising cost drivers, with significant "down payments," near- and long-term targets (10-year goal of about 60% debt ratio), and credible enforcement procedures.

---

[4]Lydia Saad. "Americans Believe GOP Should Consider Tea Party Ideas," January 31, 2011. Available at www.gallup.com/poll/145838/americans-believe-gop-consider-tea-party-ideas.aspx (accessed March 25, 2011).
[5]Scott Clement. "Tea Party Support Stable, but Interest Is Waning," April 15, 2012. Available at www.washingtonpost.com/blogs/behind-the-numbers/post/tea-party-support-stable-but-interest-is-waning/2012/04/14/gIQAPXyKHT_blog.html (Accessed September 15, 2012).

4. *Can U.S. policymakers learn from other countries that have*
    successfully utilized fiscal policy to bolster their economies?

Sure. A number of OECD [Organisation for Economic Cooperation and Development]
countries have sworn off the "deficit Kool-Aid," and significantly reduced their debt
ratios in the last decade. The Oceanics, some of the Scandinavians, Switzerland, and
The Netherlands are recent examples.

The next chapter examines the long-held argument that deficits do not
matter. That side of the debate argues that deficits are of no concern to the
health of the U.S. economy. Among their arguments include the following:

- A popular way to measure the deficit level, the deficit-to-
  GDP ratio, is predicted to decline in the future.

- Treasury securities can be issued continually to finance
  the government's needs, so paying down the debt is not
  imperative.

- Many countries are in a deficit spending mode to ride out
  the global downturn. The United States is not unique in
  its deficit situation.

- Some countries—such as Switzerland, Sweden, and
  Canada—not only have utilized deficit spending but are
  currently showing fiscal strength in a less-than-stellar
  economy.

- Treasury securities used to finance the debt are a major
  investment vehicle in the United States, supply a benchmark indicator for use by bankers, and are an essential
  component in employing monetary policy.

Read on as we explore these arguments supporting deficit spending.

Deficits Do Not Matter

There are economists, business people, politicians, and citizens who maintain that deficits do not matter. Here we'll explore the viewpoint of those who maintain that deficits are of no great concern to the health of the U.S. economy. Some, in fact, endorse deficit spending and financing as a positive economic strategy for the United States.

Public Goods Are a Priority

Deficit financing is often employed to provide goods and services that are essential to citizens. These are referred to as *public goods*. Public goods are classified as both *nonrival*—when a good or service is used by one person, others are not deprived from using it—and *nonexcludable*, when one person cannot exclude others from using the good or service. National defense (see Figure 6-1), flood control, and the legal system are all examples of public goods.

Figure 6-1. The government provides public goods such as national defense. The military personnel pictured are firefighters from the 374th Civil Engineer Squadron and members of the 374th Medical Operations Squadron. They are practicing triage during an emergency management exercise at Yokota Air Base, Japan, on February 4, 2011. *Source: U.S. Air Force, photo by Osakabe Yasuo.*

Many people can use public goods without interfering with someone else's use. Furthermore, it is difficult to prevent others from using the good or service. Flood control is a good example. Flood-control service benefits everyone in a certain locale, and providing it only to those who would pay for it is impossible. When a community protects one area from flooding, it protects everyone in that area. Consequently, this service is provided by the government as part of its role as a public goods provider.

The free-rider problem is the reason why public goods are provided by the government and not by private companies. No private firm would have an interest in providing flood control because there would be many free riders, people who would benefit from the service but would not pay.

Private goods, by contrast, are both rival and excludable. Your fast-food sandwich is a rival good because it is purchased only by you and is consumed by you. After you eat the sandwich, it is not available for anyone else's consumption. If you do not have money to pay for the sandwich, the fast-food chain excludes you from receiving the meal. Many goods in our society are private goods provided by businesses and people in the free market.

The government also provides a number of goods and services that fall between the public and private classifications. These are called *quasi-public* or *near-public goods*. The government considers these goods or services either necessary or beneficial to citizens. They have some characteristics of a public good, and some characteristics of a private good. In other words, they do not meet the full requirements of nonrival and nonexcludable. This could include a public park that charges an admittance fee (see Figure 6-2), or a highway that charges a toll for use.

Figure 6-2. The government provides many goods that are quasi-public, such as parks like Mount Rushmore National Memorial. People are charged a fee to visit the national park, located in the Black Hills of South Dakota. The 60-foot heads of Presidents George Washington, Thomas Jefferson, Theodore Roosevelt, and Abraham Lincoln are sculpted into a granite mountain. *Source: National Parks Service.*

The government also provides *merit goods* (again, often through deficit spending), which are goods and services that are provided by the government free of charge because they are socially desirable and society does not produce enough on its own. These goods and services are commonly referred to as merit goods because they hold special merit for taxpayers. Typically, these types of goods have positive externalities—third-party benefits for a society, even though not every person is using the good or service. Some examples are museums, education, health immunizations, and low-income housing for senior citizens.

Generally speaking, the spillover effects (secondary effects to those not taking part in the economic activity) to third parties, those who are not directly involved in the transactions, are not realized but are still actually so great that more of the merit goods should be produced. For example, you will benefit if your neighbor attends college. You might not think so, and you won't take his tests for him or attend classes, but you will still benefit. He may discover some great medical advancement or energy-saving technology that will benefit all consumers. Or he might start a new business that boosts economic activity in your city. Therefore, the government supports more merit goods—including educational funding—to create more third-party positive externalities. Deficit spending is sometimes necessary to include these merit goods in the national budget.

Not all externalities are positive, such as smoking, littering, and pollution. If a cost is incurred by a third party who is not directly involved in the transaction, a negative externality is incurred. Air pollution is a negative externality because living near a company's polluting factory and being exposed to pollutants can harm one's health. This neighbor may not buy any of the company's products and may just be an innocent recipient of the effects of the company's pollution. Negative externalities are costly to society but not to individual businesses. Consequently, the government tends to regulate, tax, or fine negative externalities so less will be produced. In the case of air pollution, tactics to reduce emissions include regulating and taxing companies and issuing tradable pollution permits.

Public goods, quasi-public goods, and merit goods are often associated with positive spillover effects. But controlling for negative externalities is also an important role for the government, and this, too, forces the deficit upward.

As our economy has evolved, it has devoted more resources to public goods, quasi-public goods, and merit goods. Prior to the 1930s and 1940s, most of the goods and services provided by the government were strictly public goods, such as national defense, the legal system, and the postal service. Our country had a laissez-faire philosophy, meaning that most of society was free from government intervention. But since the Great Depression, to prevent such widespread devastation from ever occurring again, government involvement in many areas has become much more prevalent. Americans have come to expect a host of services to be provided by the government, and spending beyond the strict public goods arena has become the norm. Our government uses deficit financing to furnish the goods and services our society has become accustomed to—safe highways, police protection, unemployment compensation, health care services, energy conservation programs, low-cost school lunches, regulated communication and broadcast airwaves, pollution control, and much more. If you pay attention, you'll notice the services provided by our government exist almost everywhere you go. And it's no wonder why: prior to entering World War II in 1941, U.S. government spending was just under 12 percent of GDP, while today it has doubled to over 25 percent.

As a society, we have to this point more or less agreed that some spending on public goods and merit goods is worth going into debt for—that the benefits outweigh the costs. Many economists and pundits would concur, pointing out that we have done this for years and the country is a better place for it. The flip side is that the spending has become prevalent, excessive, and indulgent. Many believe government spending must be reduced to a bare bones, minimum level, in line with society's basic needs.

Deficit Spending: A Useful Tool During a Crisis

In countries around the world and throughout recent history, it has been standard practice to deficit finance during times of crisis. During wartime, for example, needed goods and services are provided through deficit spending. As you read in Chapter 2, the United States raised funds in preparation for World War I by selling Liberty Bonds. The war debt climbed to $25 million by the end of the war. Fast-forward to WWII; according to the Bureau of the Public Debt, U.S. participation was extremely costly at $323 billion. The United States paid for military expenses and also lent funds to Britain and other countries fighting Germany, and to do so took on debt of $211 billion.[1]

As financing for wars shows, we as a nation have been able to rack up large deficits, and the wartime production spending spurs economic expansion.

Spending to pull out of an economic glut—a situation in which we have an excess of goods and services available—or a recession also falls under the category of crisis spending. During a recession, deficit spending may be a great way to boost aggregate demand and reinvigorate the economy. When the government spends money, output is stimulated and a multiplier effect in the economy occurs. Government spending increases economic activity in a greater proportion than the amount spent, creating income and job opportunities. For example, if the government builds a highway, it creates jobs for many workers on the project. Those workers, in turn, will purchase groceries, new homes, clothing, and cars. In this example, the supermarket, homebuilder, retail store, and auto industry are all stimulated. Workers at these establishments will now be able to spend, and thus restart the cycle. Deficit spending can be necessary and even beneficial for the United States during crisis situations.

Reasonable Deficit-to-GDP Ratio

A popular way to view the deficit issue is to measure the level of the annual deficit relative to GDP (gross domestic product), or the output level of the economy. In 2011, U.S. GDP stood at just over $14 trillion and the deficit totaled $1.3 trillion, resulting in a deficit-to-GDP ratio of roughly 9 percent. According to the Congressional Budget Office (CBO) baseline projections in its January 2011 *Budget and Economic Outlook: Fiscal Years 2011 to 2021*, the deficit-to-GDP ratio is expected to fall notably in the future. Deficits are

---

[1] TreasuryDirect Kids, "The History of U.S. Public Debt: The New Deal (1933-1936) to World War II (1939-1945)," www.treasurydirect.gov/kids/history/history_ww2.htm (accessed February 6, 2011).

expected to fall to 7 percent of GDP in 2012 and to 3.2 percent by 2021. Contrast that with 1943, when the deficit-to-GDP ratio totaled just over 30 percent. Even with a high ratio, the WWII era was a period of prosperity for the U.S. economy. As a society, we know that the sky does not fall if deficits are huge. The fact that benchmark numbers have been very high in the past suggests that current lower ranges indicate no need for concern.

Ricardian Equivalence Suggests Deficits Don't Matter

Some concur with an old-time economic theory, the Ricardian equivalence, named after English economist David Ricardo (1772–1823). The Ricardian equivalence says, simply, that budget deficits do not lead to a change in aggregate demand. People know that deficit borrowing needs to be repaid. The government can borrow today but will need to tax tomorrow to pay for its borrowing. Anticipating a tax increase, people increase their savings in response to a rise in deficit spending. Challenges do exist in properly measuring people's behavioral responses to deficit spending, and many economists debate the constraints underlying this theory. Nevertheless, others contend this theory is powerful "food for thought" regarding taxpayers' response to deficit spending and is a close approximation to our real-world actions.

It Isn't Necessary to Pay Down the Debt

Another common argument by proponents in the discussion of deficit spending is that the debt does not need to be paid down. As old debt matures, the U.S. Treasury will pay off existing securities. And as the deficit situation calls for more funding, the Treasury will issue more securities. Furthermore, interest rates are at historically low levels, and it is a great time for the government to borrow on the cheap. As a matter of fact, debt is a way of life for many other countries, and deficit financing is high in most of the advanced countries around the world (not with standing the threat of a real debt crisis, such as recently occurred in Greece, that made it impossible to roll over the debt, something we'll discuss in the next chapter). Congress can increase the debt limit, and Treasury Securities ("Treasuries") can be issued continually to finance the government's needs and fiscal programs. Those who argue deficits don't matter say it isn't necessary to pay down the debt, and we shouldn't worry about it. They argue that the debt can be rolled over indefinitely.

Table 6-1 outlines the deficit situation for the general government of the major advanced economies. For comparison purposes, the table contrasts the yearly budget deficits to GDP. Projections by the International Monetary Fund (IMF) show the top numbers in 2011. Japan is number one on the list with a deficit 10.1 percent of GDP, followed by the United States at 9.6 percent of GDP.

All of the major advanced economies ran budget deficits for 2011. Budget deficits averaged 6.2 percent of GDP. And although the 2015 deficit projections indicate moderation for all major countries, the forecast is a continuing deficit financing trend. These figures suggest that other developed countries are in the same deficit spending mode as the United States. Many governments are deficit spending to get through the global downturn. Because the United States is not unique in this pattern, there is no need for worry.

Table 6-1. Major Advanced Economies: Deficit Projections for General Government (in percentage of GDP)

	2011	2015
Japan	−10.1	−7.6
United States	−9.6	−4.4
United Kingdom	−8.7	−3.6
France	−5.3	−2.2
Canada	−4.5	−1.5
Italy	−3.9	−1.5
Germany	−1.0	−0.2

Source: International Monetary Fund, World Economic Outlook, April 2012.

LEARN FROM OTHERS

The United States could learn a lesson from other economies that have successfully utilized deficit spending while doing a fiscal about-face. Three good examples are Switzerland, Sweden, and Canada. All have achieved fiscal discipline. Switzerland is the cream of the crop of fiscal discipline, and a prime example of what to do. Burdened by rising deficits, in 2001, Switzerland voted in a "debt brake" provision that was adopted in 2003. The rule states the government's budget must balance, adjusted for cyclical conditions over a multiyear period. So whenever bad times hit, recessions are allowed, but surpluses must exist during a rising economy. In 2003, the debt of Switzerland was reduced from 68% to roughly 48% of GDP. Today, Switzerland has a deficit of just 0.2 of GDP.

Sweden hit some very hard economic times 20 years ago with debt as a percentage of GDP hitting the 60 to 70 percent marks. Today, the country's debt has dropped to 36 percent of GDP. And although the deficit as a percentage of GDP hit 11.8 percent in 1993, Sweden now bounces between small surpluses and small deficits. A small deficit to GDP is expected for 2012, and the country is expected to be in the surplus area by 2014. How did this happen? They followed a tough fiscal consolidation program, including a main rule requiring a surplus equal to 1 percent of GDP on average over the business cycle.

Just like the United States, Canada implemented a stimulus program during the most recent recession. But unlike the United States, Canada has recovered well. The International Monetary Fund projects that by 2017, the deficit as a percentage of GDP will be almost nil at 0.5. What made the difference? Canada adopted a modest stimulus program, easing taxes and implementing no new major programs during the recession. Canada has a long track record of fiscal discipline. When the economy entered the 2008 recession, it was in a position of fiscal strength with modest surpluses.

Treasuries Are a Savings Vehicle

Another advantage of deficit financing is that it provides a huge savings vehicle for investors. To finance deficit spending in the United States, the Bureau of the Public Debt issues Treasuries and U.S. Savings Bonds. Both are essential investments, savings instruments, and at the heart of the U.S. financial community. Because they are defined as riskless securities, they are an important part of an investment portfolio for risk-adverse consumers who prefer low volatility. Further, the majority of interest payments are made domestically, and that money remains in the United States to stimulate the economy.

Treasuries are marketable securities. They can be sold in the secondary market quickly and easily, right after purchase. So, for whatever reason or need, if an investor wants to generate funds, Treasuries are easy to sell. The Bureau of the Public Debt recently opened the investment market even wider, lowering the minimum investment in Treasuries from $1,000 to $100.

U.S. Savings Bonds are nonmarketable and traditionally have been given as gifts for life events such as graduations, weddings, and births. They are called "nonmarketable" because they are registered to a specific person and can't be traded in the secondary market. Many American workers consider them an important part of their employee savings plan, allocating a portion of their paycheck to buy Savings Bonds. Savings Bonds can be purchased for as little as $25.

Clearly, Treasuries and U.S. Savings Bonds are important consumer savings and investment avenues, as U.S. debt held by the public, in Treasuries and Savings Bonds, totals $11 trillion. These securities are guaranteed by the full faith and credit of the U.S. government, which has never defaulted. Thus, these securities are considered a risk-free investment, though they won't always maintain their full value due to inflation (excluding TIPS, Treasury Inflation-Protected Securities, which provide a measure of inflation protection). In a risky economy, the appeal of such a sound investment may be even stronger.

Treasuries Provide a Common Index

A beneficial side effect of deficit financing is that Treasury rates provide useful benchmark interest rates for bankers. Commercial and mortgage loan officers are particularly familiar with Treasuries. Variable-rate commercial loans are widely utilized in the banking industry, and T-rates are a key component of a bank's decision making. Monthly payments, for example, are adjusted—upward or downward—depending on an index. A common index for pricing is the Treasury. Let's say you have a commercial loan tied to the prime rate (the best rate for strong, credit-worthy customers) plus the 20-year Treasury bond rate. If the prime rate is 3.25 percent and the Treasury bond rate is 2 percent this month, the rate on your loan will be 5.25 percent.

Treasuries Are Essential to Monetary Policy

Monetary policy involves the actions taken by the Federal Reserve ("the Fed") to influence credit market conditions and interest rates. Along with open-market operations, as described in Chapter 4, there are two other tools for monetary policy: changing the discount rate and adjusting reserve require-ments. Open market operations, the buying and selling of government securi-ties, are the main tool for activating monetary policy. When the Fed wants to expand the money supply and lower interest rates, it buys government securi-ties and thus increases reserves in the banking system. This allows banks to make more loans. When the Fed wants to raise interest rates, it does so by selling government securities. This restricts reserves in the banking system, reducing money supply and making rates rise.

What is the Fed's main tool used to conduct open market operations? You guessed it—Treasury securities. The government uses Treasuries to deficit finance, and these very instruments are the essential vehicle for conducting monetary policy. Since the global financial crisis, beginning in 2008, the Fed also has turned to unconventional monetary policy tools, including purchasing asset-backed securities such as mortgages. Again, we've run up deficits based on these practices for decades, while only occasionally eliminating them, and the economy usually remains strong or bounces back fairly quickly.

Now that you have read the perspective of those who say deficits do not matter, the next chapter investigates the perspective of those who say deficits do matter. With the nation's burgeoning debt, this debate has become very heated. The next chapter examines the long-standing arguments against defi-cit financing, along with some new twists, such as the argument that deficit financing increases U.S. reliance on foreign creditors. The discussion also will highlight why some feel the debt issue matters more than it did previously.

Deficits Do Matter

This chapter defends the viewpoint of those who say that deficits are a huge concern and do matter. Up to this point, you have learned that continual annual deficits have led to a massive national debt. As you'll see, there are many traditional, long-standing arguments against deficit financing, along with some newer arguments, such as those related to the dangers of an increasing reliance on foreign creditors and the risk of potential downgrades of the U.S. debt. Many economists, politicians, and citizens say the debt matters more now than it used to. Let's explore why.

Foreign Share Expands

"We owe the debt to ourselves" used to be the argument proponents of deficit financing put forth when contending that the rising national debt posed no risk. There is no need to worry, they claimed, because we are in debt only to ourselves, and repaying the debt is simply a matter of redistributing income. But things have changed. As you learned in Chapter 2, the foreign ownership of U.S. debt has risen considerably over the past few years, topping $5.3 trillion as of June 2012—about a third of the total debt outstanding. The top creditor nation China, held $1.164 trillion in treasury obligations, followed by Japan with $1.119 trillion, and the "Oil Exporters" at $261 billion. As the U.S. debt swells, the country continues to rely on oversees sources for financing. Foreign debt, at an all time high, is nearing 50 percent of total privately held debt, contrasted with 30 percent just a decade prior.

There is a marked upward trend in the amount of Treasury securities held by international investors. When this foreign-held debt eventually comes due, it is the U.S. taxpayers who will be taxed to pay off the debt. This adds to the income of foreigners, and not U.S. citizens. The United States is sending interest payments outside its borders, draining money away from the U.S. economy. Our tax dollars are being used to pay for the interest on the foreign-held debt.

The United States has been relying increasingly on the foreign sector to facilitate its trillion-dollar deficit spending scheme. So far, so good. But if foreign investors become sufficiently concerned about investing in a country with such high debt levels that they scale back their investments, the U.S. government bond market will hit a wall. Some investors, including foreign banks, prefer investments in their home country because of a higher comfort level concerning economic conditions. If the main foreign buyers of Treasuries are no longer interested in purchasing U.S. government bonds, the United States will need to entice other investors to take over this significant buying role, most likely requiring it to offer an increase in interest rates, perhaps at a substantial hike.

Again, a large amount of debt could hamper the ability of policymakers to respond to domestic and international dilemmas. The government may be unable to boost spending and cut taxes, when necessary, to expand the domestic economy. Further, a significant debt burden may hamper preparation for a crisis or limit military spending. Finally, as the Congressional Budget Office (CBO) notes, "the reduced financial flexibility and increased dependence on foreign investors that would accompany a rising debt could weaken the United States' leadership."[1]

Potential Downgrading of U.S. Debt

A downgrade of the U.S. debt could have devastating financial consequences for the overall economy. Moody's, one of the largest rating agencies, continues to rate the U.S. debt as AAA, but on September 11, 2012, warned a downgrade could be on the horizon. If budget negotiations fail to produce policies that produce a "downward trend of the ratio of federal debt to GDP over the medium term" Moody's expects to lower the rating.[2]

On August 5, 2011, Standard and Poor's made a shocking announcement concerning the U.S. government debt ratings. For the first time in history, the rating

---

[1]Congressional Budget Office. *Federal Debt and the Risk of a Fiscal Crisis,* July 27, 2010. Available at www.cbo.gov/doc.cfm?index=11659 (accessed May 17, 2011).
[2]Moody's. "'AAA/A-1+' Rating on United States of America Affirmed; Outlook Revised to Negative," September 11, 2012. Available at www.moodys.com/research/Moodys-issues-update-on-the-outlook-for-the-US-governments--PR_254944 (accessed September 15, 2012).

agency removed the country's top investment grade rating and downgraded its long-term debt to AA+, noting increased concern over the government's fiscal position.

Bond ratings are a generally accepted expression of investment risk, with AAA-level ratings indicating that an investment is the least risky and thus warrants a lower interest rate. Put another way, any downgrade in U.S. debt ratings could increase the rate of interest the United States has to pay on future debt issues.

At this point, the downgrade has had minimal impact, at best, on borrowing costs. The reason is that the Federal Reserve has been keeping rates at historically low levels, and there still is a demand for the perceived safe Treasury instruments. But further downgrades could shock rates up as more risk is associated with Treasuries.

According to S&P, "The downgrade reflects our opinion that the fiscal consolidation plan that Congress and the Administration recently agreed to falls short of what, in our view, would be necessary to necessary to stabilize the government's medium-term debt dynamics."[3] The rating agency is concerned about long-term fiscal and economic challenges.

Any additional downgrade could pack a severe blow to our national ego, as the United States has always held stellar ratings and historically reigned as the world's largest powerhouse economy. S&P analyzes 128 sovereign nations, and only a dozen or so hold its top rating, including England, Canada, and Germany. But the United States is at risk of being downgraded again unless it enacts an aggressive deficit-reduction plan. As of this writing, there has been a lot of talk and political maneuvering regarding a plan, but U.S policymakers have yet to agree on a formalized plan.

The issue at stake here is that many investment firms and institutions prefer top-rated bonds. With any downgrade, there could be a huge sell-off of U.S. government bonds. To sell future Treasuries, investors would need to be enticed with a higher interest rate. Remember the risk-return trade-off discussed in Chapter 5—to accept more risk, investors must be compensated with a higher interest rate. This would mean higher interest payments must be added to the national budget each year. Plus, if a downgrade does come, the U.S. dollar may weaken as well, as more people may want to sell the currency than buy it.

---

[3]Standard & Poor's. "United States of America Long-Term Rating Lowered to 'AA+' Political Risks, Rising Debt Burden, Outlook Negative," August 5, 2011. Available at www.standardandpoors.com/ratings/articles/en/us/?assetID=1245316529563 (accessed September 17, 2012).

Global Crisis Illustrates Dangers of High Debt

During the worldwide economic downturn of the past several years, many countries incurred high deficits because they initiated spending programs to stimulate their economies. Although some countries have been successful in stimulating output and spurring employment, the debt levels of most countries have risen, increasing the chance of sovereign defaults in countries such as Greece.

Moody's recently bumped the outlook of the entire EU from stable to negative, due to outlook downgrades for the United Kingdom, France, Germany, and The Netherlands. These countries account for 45 percent of the revenue of the EU, and there is concern over their ability to support the growing debt crisis. When an economic crisis erupts in a country, debt is downgraded, and the government loses opportunities to borrow money at a reasonable interest rate. The United States has long enjoyed a strong position as the world economic leader. Even though the United States has record deficits and a historically high national debt, concern over other countries' fiscal situations has kept up a keen interest in U.S. bonds, allowing the U.S. government to keep low the rate at which it borrows money. U.S. government bonds have long been a sought-after and safe liquid investment vehicle.

Yet is helpful to look at the debacle that downgrading has caused in the eurozone countries Portugal, Ireland, Italy, Greece, and Spain—recently grouped as PIIGS. They are significantly weaker after the latest financial downturn. These countries have been plagued with slow to no economic growth, high unemployment, fiscal austerity measures that drag on the economy, and excessive debt-to-GDP numbers. And with higher borrowing costs, it becomes much harder to bring the economy back to life. Policymakers say the United States should take heed to thwart a similar crisis. It may be challenging to envision how a major economic crisis could occur in the United States, but history has shown that it can happen.

Table 7-1 lists the five PIIGS countries, along with the United States, and their government debt as a percentage of GDP—the amount of government debt divided by the output of society. Low debt relative to GDP is preferred. A number of 100 percent means paying off the debt would require all people who are working in a particular country to apply all of their wages for the year toward the debt. All of the noted countries, with the exception of Spain, have debt-to-GDP numbers that top 100 percent, indicating they owe more in debt than they earn each year. High ratios are a sign of fiscal problems, signaling that the country may have trouble paying back their debt. And although Spain may have the lowest debt-to-GDP of its European peers, projections suggest a trend upward to the 100 percent range.

Table 7-1. Government Debt: Central Government Gross Financial Liabilities[4] As a Percentage of GDP

	2010	2011	2012
Portugal	103.2	117.6	124.3
Italy	126.5	119.7	122.7
Greece	149.6	170.0	168.8
Ireland	98.4	114.1	121.6
Spain	67.1	75.3	87.9
United States	98.3	102.7	108.6

Source: Organisation for Economic Co-operation and Development (2012), "Government debt",
Economics: Key Tables from OECD, No. 21. doi: 10.1787/gov-debt-table-2012-1-en.

Ireland's debt crisis is fairly recent. It had a good credit history up until 2007. Over the next couple of years, the country was hit with an economic downturn along with a real estate bubble, which precipitated a massive failure in the banking industry. Beginning in April 2009, the country initiated a fiscal austerity program. However, deficits remain high and markets remain skeptical that Ireland has a workable fiscal plan. Debt to GDP has risen roughly fourfold over the past 5 years and the cost of borrowing has escalated greatly, to double digits. Because Ireland's bailout package is tied to market rates, its interest cost is even higher than Portugal and Greece.

Ireland, Portugal, and Greece have received emergency loans from the EU and the International Monetary Fund. Portugal has been burdened with low competitiveness in the market and excessively high levels of government debt. The government has implemented market reforms to encourage market demand, yet investors are demanding double-digit interest rates to carry debt. The outlook on sovereign debt for Portugal is rated negative by both Moody's and Standard & Poor's.

Borrowing costs for Greece are at exceptionally high levels. When the global recession hit, Greece was already in trouble, with a debt-to-GDP ratio over 100 percent. The country had experienced years of heavy spending, even prior to the economic downturn. The debt and deficit limits are high in Greece and exceed the maximum limits set by the eurozone. According to the IMF, the country's economy is forecasted to contract 4.7 percent in 2012. Social unrest—violence, riots, and protests—in Greece is growing with the debate over fiscal austerity measures, threatening financial devastation.

---

[4]According to the Organisation for Economic Co-operation and Development, "Gross financial liabilities refer to the debt and other liabilities (short and long-term) of all the institutions in the general government sector."

Italy also has an extremely high debt-to-GDP ratio, at 122 percent. Its economy has suffered from low economic growth for many years. The Italian government has made an effort to boost spending and encourage the creation of new jobs. Yet in the throes of a double-dip recession, the country is experiencing unemployment exceeding 10 percent. There is concern in the investor community over Italy's ability to service its massive debt.

Spain had a booming economy until late in 2007, when the economy hit a steep decline due to a slowdown in construction and consumer spending. The banking industry was hit hard because of its large investment in construction loans. The government tried stimulus spending, which caused the deficit to rise over the eurozone limit. Spain's current unemployment rate reflects the lack of success that move had: over 24 percent—more than triple the rate in 2007.

Portugal, Greece, Ireland, Italy, and Spain have a major theme in common: they have overspent and overborrowed. These countries have accumulated too much debt, resulting in low or no economic growth, mass unemployment, and high interest rates. Only time will tell if all will emerge from the debt crisis. But what is known is that with such a severe debt crisis, economic recovery will be a long time in coming.

Exorbitant Interest

Assuming government debt in the United States is never repaid, the interest alone presents a huge problem. Interest payments stimulate a vicious cycle: a growing deficit leads to higher debt, which in turn increases the amount of interest payments, which in turn increases the deficit because additional interest payments must be included, which leads to even higher debt, and so on.

Growing Interest Payments

Table 7-2 shows the CBO baseline projections (keeping current laws governing taxation and spending unchanged) for the next 10 years. Net interest represents interest paid by the federal government, offset by interest collections from the public and interest received by government trust funds.

You can see the trajectory path for net interest. In 2011, net interest topped the $200 billion mark and stood at 1.5 percent of GDP. But it is expected to skyrocket, projected to jump over $300 billion in 2016. Deficits are expected to rise, bringing a large increase in debt. The CBO expects debt held by the public to climb to $13 trillion, or 71 percent of GDP, by the end of 2016. In addition, interest rates are forecast to rise from their historically low levels, so the cost of carrying the debt will increase, causing interest payments to be pushed even higher over the next 10 years. CBO projections show that dollar net interest will more than triple between 2012 and 2022, rising from $224 billion to $624 billion. And as a share of GDP, it will rise over one full percentage point over the next decade, increasing from 1.4 percent to 2.5 percent.

Table 7-2. Baseline Budget Projections

	Net Interest (in billions)	Net Interest as a Percentage of GDP
2011 actual	$227	1.5
2012	$224	1.4
2013	$231	1.5
2014	$247	1.5
2015	$282	1.6
2016	$341	1.8
2017	$402	2.0
2018	$459	2.2
2019	$513	2.4
2020	$557	2.5
2021	$590	2.5
2022	$624	2.5

Source: Congressional Budget Office, The Budget and Economic Outlook: Fiscal Years 2012 to 2022, January 2012, Table 1-3, "CBO's Baseline Budget Projections."

Opportunity Cost High

There is a huge opportunity cost associated with the interest payments. The government funds could be better spent on other goods and services that bring productive value. The interest payment on the debt represents a rising portion of GDP, the productive output of our society. It indicates that an increasing percentage of our resources will be going to cover interest. Rising interest payments will most likely make it necessary for the government to reduce spending on beneficial services such as national defense, education, and environmental protection services.

Crowding Out

In economic terms, "crowding out" traditionally refers to interest rates. Crowding out occurs when heavy government borrowing forces out private borrowing. When the government increases the deficit through spending, the demand for credit rises as the government borrows by selling Treasuries. The theory goes that the government may offer a high rate of interest to attract investors. That drives up interest rates across the board and problems develop when, at some point, businesses and individuals are unable to afford the higher rates they must pay to borrow. The rising government debt results in businesses and consumers being "crowded out" of the credit market.

The crowding out process then reduces private spending and investment. In the current economic environment, this has not been an issue. Crowding out has not occurred despite record borrowing. Why? The Federal Reserve has aggressively purchased bonds and kept interest rates at historically low levels. But although crowding out has not been a problem in this economic cycle, many say it could come to pass.

Economic Panic

Panic worldwide global crisis, devastation, turmoil—however you define it, rising deficits and the ballooning debt have the potential to result in a host of serious economic problems. In the worst case imaginable, a devastating economic panic starting in the United States would spread across the globe. Hyperinflation—rapid, severe inflation—would occur as the Fed created more dollars to pay off debts. Vital government services would be curtailed in an attempt to keep up with bond payments, disrupting the economy and causing unemployment. A stock and bond sell off on Wall Street would cause the stock market to collapse, having a huge impact on other financial markets. The United States would have trouble selling government securities and would be forced to offer high interest rates to sell what are suddenly deemed risky securities. Higher interest payments would add further to the deficit and national debt, exacerbating fiscal and economic woes.

Although most economists discount the possibility of such a scenario, the long-term financial problems associated with entitlement programs such as Social Security, Medicare, and Medicaid exacerbate the fear associated with the rising debt. These programs, because they are promised by the government and have been funded in part by workers (except Medicaid), will be challenging to modify. But change in all areas, argue many these days, is needed to restore the financial health of the country. Reliance on these entitlements by U.S. citizens, coupled with the debt trajectory pattern, increases the risk for an economic panic.

As discussed in the previous sections, as the nation's debt grows, there is the real possibility investors will lose interest in purchasing government Treasuries. The U.S. government may be pushed into a position of paying exceptionally high interest rates to attract creditors. Treasury rates are at historically low levels now, averaging below 3 percent. The Federal Reserve has been actively pursuing an expansionary monetary policy, forcing interest rates down. But many believe higher rates are looming. This would trigger a further expansion of the debt as interest rates grow.

A high level of deficit spending can lead to inflation. Today, the economy is operating at less than full employment and inflation levels are minimal. Increased federal spending and a reduction in taxes can stimulate demand, while putting upward pressure on price levels. Uncontrollable deficit spending can lead to inflation. A rise in prices has not occurred yet because the economy has considerable slack and is operating below its capacity. If the economy were operating at full capacity, then deficit spending could overstimulate the economy and spur inflation.

According to ten former members of the President's Council of Economic Advisers, in an open letter published by Politico, "These deficits will take a toll on private investment and economic growth. At some point, bond markets are likely to turn on the United States—leading to a crisis that could dwarf 2008."[5] The group of esteemed economists was commenting on the recently released bipartisan National Commission on Fiscal Responsibility and Reform report entitled "The Moment of Truth." (See Figure 7-1) The letter was designed to alert readers that the threat of the long-run budget deficit is severe and calls for "serious and prompt attention."

Figure 7-1. Members of the press cover President Barack Obama's April 14, 2011, meeting in the Oval Office with Erskine Bowles and Alan Simpson, cochairs of the National Commission on Fiscal Responsibility and Reform. President Obama created the commission to "improve the fiscal situation in the medium term and to achieve fiscal sustainability over the long run." Seated on the couch, from left, are Senator Simpson, Treasury Secretary Timothy Geithner, and Office of Management and Budget Director Jack Lew. *Source: Official White House Photo by Pete Souza.*

---

[5]*Politico.* "Unsustainable Budget Threatens Nation," March 24, 2011. Available at www.politico.com/news/stories/0311/51864.html (accessed May 16, 2011).

Limited Flexibility in a Crisis

Operating with such a high level of debt could place the United States in an extremely challenging position. It severely constrains, or limits, policymakers' fiscal policy options. If a crisis occurs, such as a new war, a terrorist attack, a banking crisis, or an economic depression or recession, the exploding deficit levels and rising debt will limit the options Congress has in responding to such a crisis. This could prove to be extremely serious, particularly if the need arose to respond to or prepare for an international incident. As noted by the CBO, "A large amount of debt could also harm national security by constraining military spending in times of crisis or limiting the ability to prepare for a crisis."[6]

The last major historical crisis was during World War II. At that time, the government had the flexibility to deficit spend, borrowing roughly $211 billion to pay for the war effort. The United States has not faced a tragedy of that magnitude since then, but at that point in history, government leaders were able to make decisions and preparations for the war effort before the United States entered the war. With the amount of debt now at a historical high, it is difficult to predict whether the United States would be in a position to act as quickly if a similar political threat occurred unexpectedly. The high debt, coupled with a heavy reliance on foreign investors, further complicates the situation for potential wartime or antiterrorist spending.

This lack of flexibility is not limited to national security issues. Even the most recent downturn (December 2007 through June 2009) was bolstered by the $787 billion American Recovery and Reinvestment Act of 2009, which at the time was economically feasible. Its intent was to restore jobs and stimulate economic growth. If another recession is on the horizon, with the deficit levels way over $1 trillion, it is questionable if policymakers would have taxpayer support to proceed with another economic stimulus package of mass proportions.

Burden to Future Generations

The burden of such a large national debt will fall to your children and their children. This is a long-time concern with the debt situation and has become increasingly important as the portion of debt held by foreigners has risen over the past few years. Let's explore the controversy by way of two scenarios.

The first scenario is that the government makes the decision to pay off the debt all it once. The government could send out a bill of $50,000—today's per capita cost to retire the debt—to each and every person in the United States. Obviously, it would be impossible for most people to pay that amount, and therefore it is not a practical way to remedy the indebtedness. That leaves

---

[6]Congressional Budget Office. *Federal Debt and the Risk of a Fiscal Crisis*, July 27, 2010. Available at www.cbo.gov/doc.cfm?index=11659 (accessed May 17, 2011).

the second scenario, repayment by future generations. In this scenario, future taxpayers will be taxed to pay off a debt that came from the deficit spending of their parents' and grandparents' generations. Looked at another way, today's taxpayers are enjoying the increased consumption of goods and services provided by the government, but their descendants must pick up the tab. Many think this is grossly unfair. Of course, there will be some potential benefits to future generations. For example, there may be a new national park, museum, or road that future generations will enjoy.

Scenario number two assumes that the debt will never be paid off. Future generations will be taxed hundreds of billions of dollars each year just to make interest payments on debt incurred by our current society. On the portion that is internally held (U.S. bondholders), this situation involves a redistribution of income from the taxpayer to the bondholder. Most taxpayers will be taxed to pay the interest on debt, while others will be receiving the interest payments as bondholders.

The external debt the portion owed to foreigners is roughly one-third of the total debt burden at this time. The interest payments going to the foreign sector represent enormous sums of money flowing out of the United States, and are a major concern to many taxpayers. This involves transferring roughly 1 percent of the country's output outside the United States. Each dollar paid in interest to foreign governments, corporations, and individuals is one dollar less that is available for U.S. outlays, such as education, environmental protection, and roads.

Promoting Fiscal Irresponsibility

As a matter of principle, most parents teach their children to budget their money and not to overspend. Managing finances wisely is an important goal, but meeting this goal can be a struggle, particularly during an economic downturn. Planning for your financial future should be a top priority. Wise money management involves setting financial goals for such things as educational expenses, retirement savings, and investments.

The financial management steps are quite simple: don't overspend and put some funds in savings each month so that you can reach your future financial goals. And, of course, if you have incurred debt, take action to pay it down. Sadly, for many people, excessive spending and personal debt has become a way of life. According to the Federal Reserve, the total consumer debt (excluding mortgages) as of July 2012 stands at an overwhelming $2.7 trillion.[7] The National

---

[7]The Federal Reserve. "Federal Reserve Statistical Release G.19: 'Consumer Credit,'" September 10, 2012. Available at www.federalreserve.gov/releases/g19/current/default.htm (accessed September 15, 2012).

Foundation for Credit Counseling recently released the 2012 Consumer Financial Literacy Survey, which shows that over one-half of adults do not have a budget, nor do they track their spending. Over one-third of Americans do not save any fraction of household income for retirement. And one-third of adults, or 77 million Americans, do not pay all their bills on time.[8]

Many people think that just as individuals and families must balance their budgets, the federal government must do the same or be held accountable for how much they are spending. Although families and the federal government are certainly not an apples-to-apples comparison, the analogy does illustrate a point. Budgetary belt tightening is often beneficial. For the past few years, the U.S. government spent over $1 trillion more than it took in. The federal government, having accrued massive debt, sets a fiscally irresponsible example for others. People, business entities, and now the federal government have become far too accustomed to uncontrolled spending. The high-level government attitude that it is okay to spend more than one makes perhaps has spilled over to the American population.

And here's an ironic twist—a so-called "pork project" that may actually improve the fiscal acumen of some. In 2010, the U.S. government invested $4,283,375 for nine financial literacy and education programs. According to the Citizens Against Government Waste, this included $3,150,000 for the financial education and prehome ownership counseling demonstration project, along with $305,875 for a national program promoting financial literacy for the Girl Scouts of the USA.[9]

Summary

For economists, politicians, and citizens who prefer a smaller government, rising deficits and exploding debt come with a high cost. Controlling the level of the debt, viewed as essential by many, will be discussed in the final chapter. It can be done through a plethora of strategies—eliminating pork projects, reforming Social Security, Medicare, and Medicaid, increasing taxes, reducing government spending, and balancing the budget. Read on to truly get a handle on the national debt.

---

[8]The National Foundation for Credit Counseling and the Network Branded Prepaid Card Association. *The 2012 Consumer Financial Literacy Survey, Final Report*, April 2012 (prepared by Harris Interactive Inc. Public Relations Research). Available at www.nfcc.org/NewsRoom/newsreleases/SIGNIFICANT_GAPS.cfm (accessed September 15, 2012).

[9]Citizens Against Government Waste. *2010 Congressional Pig Book Summary*. Available at www.cagw.org/reports/pig-book/2010/ (accessed May 14, 2011).

Get a Handle on the National Debt

If you believe that exploding deficits are a problem and the national debt is out of control, then the solution is to become informed and take control of the problem. How do we, as a society, go about that process? While virtually everyone has an opinion on the debt and its level of gravity, most would concur that there are some very basic steps the United States can take to address the rising deficits and debt. How these strategies are developed and employed can be varied, blended, and adjusted, but each will help give the United States a more sound financial footing. This chapter addresses the following topics:

- The basic formula to curb deficits
- Balancing the budget
- Eliminating pork projects
- Empowering states
- Using the debt ceiling as a tool
- Reforming entitlement programs
- Long-term planning

The chapter also highlights the example set by The Concord Coalition, an organization that has taken up the call to action and is "getting a handle" on the debt.

The Basic Formula to Curb Deficits

The formula for curbing deficits is easy to comprehend. It consists of two action items. First, the federal government can increase revenues. Its main strategy for doing this is to increase taxes. Second, the federal government can decrease spending. There is a third policy solution, which is the combination of these two—increase taxes *and* decrease spending.

The formula is easy to comprehend, but not easy to implement. Why? Obviously, increasing taxes is a politically unpopular strategy. Reducing government spending may not be well received by the public, either. People do not like to see programs and services cut, particularly if it will impact them directly. Try telling your elderly next-door neighbor that her Social Security benefits will be cut significantly. Or break the news to your friend who has been out of work for 6 months, and has a family to support, that his unemployment benefits will now be terminated. Cutting government spending poses a dilemma for politicians: the cuts are necessary, but they are not entirely popular. Although an increase in taxes, a reduction in government spending, or a combination of the two may be the best strategy for the economy, any choice could cost politicians votes.

Consider the impact of a decrease in taxes. The Bush administration tax cuts of 2001 (in the middle of a recession) and 2003 caused the economy to shift from surpluses to deficits. The tax cuts expired at the end of 2010, only to receive a 2-year extension during the presidency of Obama, a move designed to assist in the economic recovery. Those supporting the Bush tax cuts say the actions have been effective in stimulating the economy. Opponents say it was a disappointing stimulus that did not lead to stronger economic growth. What is agreed on is that when the Bush administration cut taxes, it had a large impact on the deficit.

Yet, given the fragile economy, raising taxes to reduce the deficit might not be a good idea. In a depressed economy, the effect of raising taxes could prove counterproductive to a recovery. Although the gap between revenue and spending will lessen, the result could be hard on individuals trying to survive on less disposable income. Higher taxes could therefore cause more businesses to close and further thwart an increase in GDP.

Exactly what options are available to policymakers for curbing the deficits? Surprisingly, this question has a myriad of answers. Here is just an example of budgetary changes that would put the country on sounder footing. The Congressional Budget Office (CBO) recently released a 256-page report, *Reducing the Deficit: Spending and Revenue Options,* containing 105 policy options to assist federal lawmakers in evaluating the possible implications of policy choices. This report is designed to help citizens and lawmakers examine some of the options available to reduce the debt. According to the CBO, "If current laws remain unchanged, deficits will total $7 trillion over the next decade."[1]

The options are divided into three sections in the report: reducing mandatory spending, reducing discretionary spending, and increasing revenues. Although discretionary spending is governed by Congress's annual appropriation acts, mandatory spending, also called entitlements, is funded based on certain qualifications or rules set by Congress. According to the CBO, the largest programs in this category are Social Security, Medicare, and Medicaid, which together accounted for roughly three-fourths of mandatory spending in 2010.

Table 8-1 shows just a sampling of options suggested by the CBO, demonstrating that there are many available choices for cutting spending or increasing revenues. Perhaps the most telling point from this sampling chart is that every dollar of cost savings or increased revenues really adds up. Of course, these choices are going to be politically difficult to get enacted. Who, after all, really wants to give up their mortgage deduction?

Table 8-1. Reducing the Deficit: Sample Spending and Revenue Options

Mandatory Spending/Savings (2012–2021)	Discretionary Spending/ Savings (2012–2021)	Revenues/Increase in Revenues (2012–2021)
Option 16: Reduce the floor on Federal matching rates for Medicaid services (lowering the floor would require states with higher per-capita income to be responsible for a larger share of the Medicaid program)	Option 2: Cap increases in military basic pay	Option 2: Raise tax rates on capital gains
Savings: $8.6 billion	Savings: $17.3 billion	New revenues: $48.5 billion

(continued)

[1]Congressional Budget Office. *Reducing the Deficit: Spending and Revenue Options,* March 2011. Available at www.cbo.gov/doc.cfm?index=12085 (accessed May 27, 2011).

Table 8-1. (*continued*)

Mandatory Spending/Savings (2012–2021)	Discretionary Spending/ Savings (2012–2021)	Revenues/Increase in Revenues (2012–2021)
Option 18: Raise the age of eligibility for Medicare to 67	Option 20: Limit highway funding to expected highway revenues	Option 4: Gradually eliminate the mortgage interest deduction
Savings: $125 billion	Savings: $85.6 billion	New revenues: $214.6 billion
Option 30: Raise the full retirement age in Social Security	Option 34: Increase payment by tenants in Federally assisted housing	Option 9: Include investment income from life insurance and annuities in taxable income
Savings: $119.9 billion	Savings: $25.4 billion	New revenues: $259.5 billion

Source: *Congressional Budget Office, Reducing the Deficit: Spending and Revenue Options, March 2011.*

Roughly half of outlays are discretionary, part of the annual appropriations. In 2010, for example, over half of the discretionary spending was on defense. Defense spending totaled $689 billion, largely from operations and maintenance, military personnel, and procurement. Some people feel military spending should not be touched due to safety concerns. Another side says defense cuts need to be considered while weighing the effects on military capabilities and compromise to national security. In the CBO study, 12 out of the 38 discretionary spending options focused on defense.

The CBO study points to the fact that there are many options available for deficit reduction. The choices will come from the spending side or tax policy. To secure the best deficit reduction plan, politicians should put all options on the table for discussion.

Balance the Budget

Perhaps the simplest way to get rid of budget deficits, and consequently the growth in the national debt, is to require a balanced budget. Over the past few years, with the rise of the debt limit, the discussion of having a balanced-budget amendment to the U.S. Constitution has emerged. In reality, such an amendment would be difficult to enforce because it requires balancing a future estimated budget. This means next year's estimated revenues must equal next year's estimated spending. The budget is actually balanced at the end of the fiscal year. A balanced-budget amendment would require that tough choices be made in the political arena on both the revenue and spending sides.

Back in 1997, support for a balanced-budget amendment was strong, failing by a single vote in the Senate. Although quite a few lawmakers supported a balanced budget, few economists agreed. In January of 1997, a total of 1,060 prominent economists, including 11 Nobel Prize winning economists, issued a warning statement to the president and Congress. The letter, organized by the Economic Policy Institute, said, "We condemn the proposed 'balanced-budget' amendment to the federal constitution. It is unsound and unnecessary."[2] Economists believe that a forced, balanced-budget amendment would cause harm to the U.S. economy. The rationale is that it would aggravate recessions, causing distress to an already weak economy.

Balancing the budget would require extreme budget cuts, or tax increases, or both. Generally, the problems with such a proposal become apparent when addressing the question of what to do if there is a depression or economic recession. The government would no longer be able to employ fiscal policy to stimulate the economy, because the goal and mandate would be to balance the budget. For example, if a recession hits, Congress would not be able to pass an economic stimulus package to move the economy, eliminating the opportunity to heal the recession with government spending. And in a war or other financial crisis? Without some exceptions written into the plan, annual spending on wartime production or national defense would be insufficient to take care of the country's defense or security needs. In reality, a clause allowing national security protection would be common in a balanced-budget amendment. And that might allow an escape hatch for more spending, as many things can be lumped under the heading of national security.

New discussion centering on a balanced budget emerged very recently. On March 31, 2011, a balanced-budget amendment was cosponsored by all Senate Republicans. It required the president to submit a balanced budget to Congress every year. The proposal capped government spending at 18 percent of gross domestic product, required a three-fifths vote to raise the national debt limit, and required a two-thirds vote to raise taxes. It also allowed exceptions for declarations of war and situations involving a military threat.

This amendment contained strong reforms that severely curtailed the ability to implement fiscal policy and thwart a recovery. Recall from Chapter 1 that automatic stabilizers are designed to offset fluctuations in the economy

---

[2]Economic Policy Institute. "Over 1000 Economists Oppose Balanced Budget Amendment, Warning It Is 'Unsound and Unnecessary,'" news release. Available at www.ombwatch.org/files/bba/econ.html (accessed June 21, 2011).

without direct intervention from Congress. When the economy weakens, for example, unemployment payments rise as more people lose their jobs. This extra money provides a boost to the economy and helps ease the downturn. It also causes government spending to rise. With a balanced-budget amendment, automatic stabilizers such as unemployment compensation would be limited. The amendment proposal was largely seen as a symbolic vote to highlight the growing public concern over the deficit, and on November 18, 2011, it was defeated in the House.

The Concord Coalition

The management of the federal budget and deficits is a challenging and complex public policy issue. In an effort to keep the federal debt from become unsupportable by our nation, one organization—The Concord Coalition—has given the public a voice and taken on the mission of fiscal reform. Harry Zeeve, the National Field Director of The Concord Coalition, answered some questions regarding the educational role of this nationwide organization, the federal debt, its consequences for the future, and the role of concerned citizens.

What is the mission of The Concord Coalition?

We are a nonpartisan, grassroots organization founded in 1992, with the mission of challenging elected officials to make the tough political choices required to balance the budget and keep it balanced over the long term. Cochaired by former Senators Warren B. Rudman (R-NH) and Bob Kerrey (D-NE), The Concord Coalition is dedicated to changing the political climate by standing up for generationally responsible fiscal policy, honestly balanced federal budgets, increased national savings, equitable Social Security and Medicare reform, and higher standards of living for future generations of Americans. Our staff of budget experts in Washington provides data, analysis, and a nonpartisan perspective for news media, interested citizens, elected officials, and others. At the same time, our field staff members stationed around the country speak to many different organizations, work with our volunteers, and encourage more people to become engaged in fiscal reform.

Why do deficits and debt matter, and why should we care?

Large chronic deficits matter because:

- Deficits lower future economic growth by reducing national savings.

- Deficits increase our dependence on foreign lenders who may not always have our best interests at heart.

- Deficits increase the burdens on future generations through rising debt service costs and fewer productivity-enhancing investments.

- Deficits raise uncertainty about future government policies.

- Deficits reduce the government's flexibility to deal with unexpected developments such as war, recession, and other emergencies.

Ignoring these consequences will imperil the well-being of future generations. Ultimately, our economy is not growing fast enough to keep up with the government's growing debt. Rising health care costs and an aging population will create massive shortfalls that could damage the economy and lower living standards unless we can put the country on a more responsible fiscal path.

What can an individual, who is concerned about rising deficits and debt, do?

Public understanding and engagement are vital in finding solutions. The Concord Coalition depends on the initiative of concerned citizens to carry the message of fiscal responsibility forward. Telling your representative and senators that you support fiscal reform and generational responsibility is essential. So is letting them know that everything—spending and taxes—must be "on the table" to help rein in future deficits. Individuals can help bring others into the national discussion by organizing speeches, educational exercises, forums, and meetings with members of Congress. Learning about the issues and leading the discussion with friends, family, and your community and social media networks are at the heart of what everyone can do to ensure that future generations of Americans enjoy economic prosperity.

Eliminate Pork Projects

Most people would agree that our government spends money on many beneficial and much-needed goods and services. Occasionally, though, the spending gets out of control, which many people would argue has been the case over the past few years. While the economy has taken a dip and the revenue stream has fallen, government spending has increased, causing a widening of the gap. Spending is often buried in unrelated legislation, with many politicians in Congress sending chunks of the annual federal budget back to their home districts and states to promote local self-interests, and therefore improve their re-election status. This type of spending is sometimes referred to as "pork-barrel spending"—government money spent in a particular locale that brings advantages to its political representative. The projects funded by this spending are known as "pork projects." One way to trim the deficit is to cut out the pork!

Citizens Against Government Waste (CAGW) is a private, nonpartisan, nonprofit organization with over one million members. As a taxpayer watchdog, the group has many publications highlighting wasteful spending, including the well-known annual *Congressional Pig Book*. In the 2010 edition of the book, a total of 9,129 pork projects were identified, at a cost of $16.5 billion, in the 12 Appropriations Acts for fiscal 2010.[3] Compared to the nearly $16 trillion national debt, $16.5 billion may not seem like much money. Certainly, some

---

[3]Citizens Against Government Waste, *2010 Congressional Pig Book Summary*, www.cagw.org/reports/pig-book/2010/ (accessed May 28, 2011).

projects classified as pork, such as the $300,000 youth-soccer program aimed at gang prevention, may be worthwhile, even life-changing, initiatives. But it is pork-barrel spending as a whole that sets a poor example of unrestrained spending. The following are some programs identified as pork by CAGW:

- $26,360,000 for a fitness facility at Mayport Naval Station

- $4,900,000 to cover seven projects for smart grid technology, the purpose of which is to reduce waste

- $3,150,000 for a financial education and prehome ownership counseling demonstration project

- $2,573,000 for potato research in four states, requested by five senators and four representatives

According to the 2012 *Pig Book*:

> The good news is that the number and cost of earmarks have decreased dramatically since fiscal year (FY) 2010, when the last Pig Book was published. The number has dropped by 98.3 percent, from 9,129 in FY 2010 to 152 in FY 2012. The cost has decreased by 80 percent, from $16.5 billion in FY 2010 to $3.3 billion in FY 2012, which is the lowest amount since 1992.[4]

This, of course, has more to do with Congressional gridlock leading up to the 2012 elections, but many hail it as a step in the right direction.

Even politicians who are well-intentioned and want keep the reins on fiscal spending may fall prey to pork. Bill writers often bury pork projects of lawmakers in the spending bill. One politician who makes it his mission to watch for wasteful spending is Oklahoma Republican Senator Tom Coburn. Coburn puts out an annual *Wastebook*. In 2010, Coburn identified in his report $11.5 billion worth of 100 wasteful pork projects, some of which are real shockers. Taxpayers got hit with a bill of $615,000 to make the Grateful Dead's archives free and available to the public. Congress spent $28.5 million to print the rarely used paper versions of the Congressional Record, which is also available online. The National Science Foundation directed $239,000 to a study on Internet dating.[5]

[4]Citizens Against Government Waster, *2012 Congressional Pig Book Summary*, www.cagw.org/reports/pig-book/2012/ (accessed September 15, 2012).
[5]Tom Coburn. *Wastebook 2010: A Guide to Some of the Most Wasteful Government Spending of 2010*, December 2010. Available at www.coburn.senate.gov/public// index.cfm?a=Files.Serve&File_id=4a184ddb-cd85-4052-b38b-5a1116acca8c (accessed May 27, 2011).

Empower States

A philosophical debate emerged in the recent financial crisis on the appropriate balance of power between the federal and state governments. Maintaining a smaller federal government by shifting additional power to states is one option for handling the national debt and deficit situation. The federal government taxes businesses and individuals in each state, then appropriates and administers the funds back to the state level for specific projects. Many of these items are politically motivated pork projects benefiting select states, while others come with high regulatory costs. A simple mandate of keeping funds closer to home and allowing states to handle taxation needs to carry such projects, could have a beneficial impact on the country's bottom line. States may, after all, understand the needs of their constituents better and can devise and administer traditional pass-through allocations such as arts and cultural programs and job creation services. The federal government would thus be allowed to focus on projects that have the larger national focus, such as defense and agriculture.

Debt Ceiling a Useful Tool

The statutory limit on the amount of federal debt is often referred to as the *debt ceiling*. It is a figure set by Congress as the maximum amount of borrowing allowed by the federal government. The number is an arbitrary credit limit set by Congress, causing some to say that the ceiling has no credibility. Regardless, the government cannot legally exceed this debt ceiling without defaulting on its loans. Congress has prevented this from occurring by periodically raising the statutory limit.

Historical Debt Limit

Placing a statutory limit on the amount of national debt began with the Second Liberty Bond Act of 1917. Prior to this time, Congress had to authorize each sale of government debt. The $11.5 billion limit set in 1917 allowed the Treasury to issue long-term Liberty Bonds within that range, which helped with the financing of World War I. The debt limits over the next two decades also set separate caps for various types of debt. The debt limit was $45 billion in 1939, when Congress created the first aggregate limit that covered nearly all of public debt, according to the Congressional Research Service.[6]

---

[6]D. Andrew Austin and Mindy R. Levit. "The Debt Limit: History and Recent Increases," January 28, 2010 (Congressional Research Service Report for Congress No. RL31967). Available at assets.opencrs.com/rpts/RL31967_20100128.pdf (accessed May 28, 2011).

The debt ceiling has been debated and raised numerous times since then, but there have been some more memorable mile markers. In 1945, the debt ceiling was raised to $300 billion for ease in financing costs for World War II. The debt limit was increased to just under $1 trillion in 1980. Move forward to February 12, 2010, when it was increased to $14.3 trillion. That is a fourteen-fold increase in the past 30 years.

Debt Ceiling Crisis

The debate over the debt ceiling became widespread and serious in spring of the following year. According to Treasury Secretary Tim Geithner, the U.S. government would be unable to pay its bills beginning on August 2, 2011, if the debt ceiling was not increased. This remark brought a debate in Congress over the issue of rising and long-term deficits. Republicans pushed for slashes in spending, in exchange for their yes votes, for the debt ceiling hike. Eventually, a complicated agreement was reached and signed by President Obama on the same day the money was to run out. The debt ceiling was raised from $14.3 trillion to $16.4 trillion, in two stages, while reducing budget deficits by at least $2.1 trillion over the next 10 years.

It definitely incites fear when the national debt nears the ceiling. The discussion and debate in Congress begins anew over whether the debt limit should be raised and, if so, by how much. Congress has always—eventually—increased the limit when the debt amount approached the ceiling. If the government did not raise the limit, it would cause huge financial turmoil because the United States would then default on many of its obligations. Implications of a default would be potentially severe with possible ramifications including, among others, an interruption of critical governmental operations, a loss of political clout among nations, and huge sell-off of stocks on Wall Street. The United States would have difficulty selling Treasuries and would need to offer a very high interest rate to entice investors to hold the risky securities. The extra interest burden would further exacerbate the national debt.

Sometimes a budget impasse does result in a temporary government shutdown. A budget impasse between President Bill Clinton and Republican leaders led to partial government shutdowns in 1995 and 1996, which lasted 28 days in total. Although not related to the debt limit, the event did foreshadow some of the pain a debt-ceiling fallout would bring. Thousands of nonessential federal workers were furloughed, and government parks, museums, and offices were closed. Congress no doubt remembers the debacle and will likely work to avoid another shutdown.

Limit Makes Us Mindful of the Deficit

The debt ceiling, which has been around for nearly a century, forces politicians to be mindful of government spending and revenue. If nothing more, the limit may function as a useful tool—a wise check and balance. The political discussions and news coverage reverberate to taxpayers, putting more pressure on politicians to be fiscally responsible. Taxpayers should assist lawmakers in taking account of the fiscal situation of the country. If you feel strongly about the debt ceiling, one way or another, be sure to write or e-mail your lawmakers.

Reform Entitlement Programs

Mandatory spending (displayed in Figure 8-1) accounts for over half of federal outlays. The largest programs in this group are Social Security, Medicare, and Medicaid. These three entitlement programs together accounted for 74 percent of mandatory spending in fiscal year 2010. As part of the budget, these entitlement programs are growing faster than any other line item, and are projected to account for an incredible 81 percent of mandatory spending by 2021, based on current law.

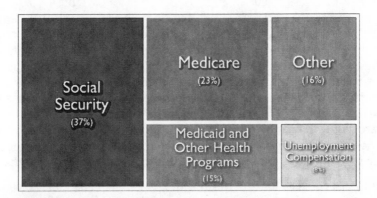

Figure 8-1. Breakdown of mandatory spending in 2010. *Source: Congressional Budget Office, "Reducing the Deficit: Spending and Revenue Options," March 2011.*

This problem is only going to get worse in the coming years, with the aging of the baby boomer population and the associated growth in health care costs as they reach retirement age. Social Security, Medicare, Medicaid, and other health care programs are expected to increase from 9.9 percent of total GDP in 2010, to 12.0 percent by 2021. This increase is heavily attributed to rapid growth in health care costs, according to a recent study by the CBO.[7]

To reduce the budget deficit significantly in the short and long term, the growth of federal mandatory spending must be restrained. The CBO suggests several possible approaches to reducing such spending. First of all, policymakers could modify the automatic indexation of benefits, by using a different index or inflation adjustor. An adjustment could potentially result in huge cost savings as mandatory programs typically use some type of indexing for inflation to set the annual change in benefits. Another option is to alter which populations are entitled to certain benefits or increase eligibility age requirements. Last, policymakers could reduce the federal government's share of spending for certain programs.[8]

Retirement, Health Care, and the Deficit

The majority of politicians seem to agree that the United States has a serious debt problem. The political debate is centered on finding the best options to reverse direction and place the deficit on a downward trend. There are many opinions within Congress, but there does seem to be a large consensus that we must move forward with proposals to alter entitlement programs.

Many proposals to reduce the deficit are focused on the largest U.S. entitlement program, Social Security, at $701 billion in outlays during 2010. They include changing the retirement age for Social Security and increasing the Social Security payroll tax base. "Thinking outside the box" may be required to sustain entitlement programs, such as the controversial 2012 budget plan introduced by Representative Paul Ryan (R-WI), which would trim the deficit by $4.4 trillion over the next decade. A highly debated and ambitious deficit reduction plan, it includes huge government spending cuts, totaling $6.2 trillion over the next 10 years. It contains drastic changes to Medicaid and Medicare, but it does not overhaul Social Security.[9] Yet it does require that if Social Security is not sustainable, the president and Congress must legislate a plan for solvency. (You can read more about the Ryan plan in Appendix C.)

Another huge concern for Americans is the long-term impact that Obamacare will have on the deficit. The CBO estimates that the Patient Protection and

---

[7]Congressional Budget Office. *Reducing the Deficit: Spending and Revenue Options*, March 2011. Available at www.cbo.gov/doc.cfm?index=12085 (accessed May 27, 2011).
[8]Ibid.
[9]Paul Ryan. "The Path to Prosperity: Restoring America's Promise, Fiscal Year 2012 Budget Resolution," Report to House Committee on the Budget. Available at budget.house.gov (accessed June 24, 2011).

Affordable Care Act of 2010 (PPACA) will, on net, actually shrink the deficit over the next 10 years rather than expand it.

Challenges Facing Social Security

As mentioned in Chapter 1, this federally funded retirement program is particularly problematic now because the baby boomer generation is starting to reach retirement age. Further, people are living longer than ever before. According to U.S. Census Bureau projections, the average life expectancy at birth was 70.8 years in 1970, but it is projected to be 78.9 years in 2015 and 79.5 years in 2020.[10] The exhaustion of the Social Security Trust Fund is on the horizon. As a larger portion of the U.S. population enters retirement and the number of people in the work force is reduced, the trust fund balances will gradually be depleted in the late 2030s. At the end of 2010, there were 54 million people who received social security benefits, while 157 million people were paying into the fund. According to one long-range estimate, by 2035 there will be 91 million people receiving benefits with 187 million workers covered by the program.[11]

Let's explore the age extension and payroll tax options from the CBO report *Reducing the Deficit: Spending and Revenue Options* (March 2011), introduced earlier in the chapter. Currently, the earliest age to start receiving Social Security retirement payments is 62 years old. According to the CBO report, about 40 percent of the population chooses this early option, with the majority claiming benefits by age 66. People who opt to take benefits before the full retirement age (now age 66, and changes to age 67 for people born in 1960 and later) receive less than full benefits each month, although they do get benefits for a longer period. The CBO proposal suggests raising the earliest age for retirement to 64 (for those born after 1960). This would save $143.9 billion over the next 10 years. Those in favor of this option point out that because of longer life expectancy, people should work to a later age.

Another plan, upping the full retirement age (the age at which one receives full benefits), is a highly impactful strategy to reduce the deficit. Workers born before 1960 can currently receive full Social Security benefits at age 66. The

[10]U.S. Census Bureau. Statistical Abstract of the United States: 2011, Table 102, "Expectation of Life at Birth, 1970 to 2007, and Projections, 2010 to 2020." Available at www.census.gov/compendia/statab/2011/tables/11 s0103.pdf (accessed June 16, 2011).
[11]Board of Trustees. *The 2011 Annual Report of the Board of Trustees of the Federal Old-Age and Survivors Insurance and Federal Disability Insurance Trust Funds*, May 13, 2011, Washington, DC: Government Printing Office. Available at www.ssa.gov/oact/TR/2011/ (accessed June 16, 2011).

CBO suggests raising the age at which workers born in 1973 or later become eligible for full retirement to 70. This would trim spending by $119.9 billion, making the total savings from age adjustments near $264 billion.

Social Security is financed by payroll taxes on employers, employees, and self-employed individuals. Wages earned, up to a maximum level, are subject to the payroll tax. In 2011, the maximum earnings subject to Social Security payroll tax is $106,800. Each year the maximum cap goes up, based on an index. A third proposal by the CBO is to raise the taxable maximum for Social Security to $170,000 in 2012 and beyond. This would mean more money coming into the Social Security system, increasing revenues by $467.8 billion over the next 10 years. Based on this option, the Social Security Trust Fund would not be depleted until after 2050.

BEWARE THE "FISCAL CLIFF"

As part of the agreement to raise the debt ceiling by $2.1 trillion to $16.4 trillion, $900 billion in savings over the next ten years comes from discretionary spending caps. Additionally, a bipartisan supercommittee was created to reach a deal on cuts totaling at least $1.2 trillion over 10 years. If the committee failed to reach a deal, at the beginning of 2013, automatic cuts to domestic spending and defense programs would be triggered.

Guess what? The country is now teetering on a fiscal cliff, falling into economic disaster unless Congress intercedes because the supercommittee did not reach a deal. Employers in the defense industry, where half of the cuts will eventually take place—$55 billion in 2013 alone—are already preparing for huge layoffs.

With the stipulated spending cuts and Bush-era tax cuts expiring, this means double trouble for an already stagnant economy, potentially pushing the United States into a double-dip recession. Policy makers must prepare a long-term, credible, deficit reduction plan, not a short-term austerity measure. A plan should be devised to reduce the deficit gradually, to avoid further damage to the weathered U.S. economy.

Conclusions

You now should be able to answer the question posed by this book's title, "Why should I care about the deficit?" Fortunately, the topic of the deficit and debt has taken center stage lately, causing more people to become concerned. As you've now seen, deficit spending can be a useful tool. It can accommodate great flexibility for our country's needs—paying for wars, supplying additional funds during a fiscal crisis, providing a safety net for U.S. citizens, and pulling the economy out of a recession, among other benefits.

But as you've also seen, the deficit and resulting total debt also has the potential to throw the United States into economic turmoil and fiscal crisis. It needs to be controlled and managed carefully.

Although the economic situation may seem dire to many, the United States can still get the debt under control to avoid many of the negative consequences. As a nation, we have the knowledge and capability to manage the debt and come out economically stronger. The key to managing the deficit and debt is to take action now to put the nation on a stronger economic path for the future.

Voice Your Opinion on the Debt

It's a typical pattern for the economy to move through cyclical highs and lows. This is referred to as a *business cycle*. The marketplace will not always move at a full-throttle pace. At times, the stock market will dip, business profits will stagnate, unemployment will rise, and consumer confidence will falter. The economy will move through peaks and troughs, or highs and lows.

You have no doubt heard the adage, "You have to have bad times to appreciate the good times." This saying holds true with the economy. It will eventually correct itself. The stock market will improve. Businesses will streamline, and profits will rise. A more efficient and stronger job market will emerge. Consumers will become bullish on the economy and start to spend again. This cycle of repeating highs and lows is a natural fluctuation, consisting of slowdowns followed by pickups in the economy. Government fiscal actions and central bank monetary policy may be used to even out, speed up, or slow down the fluctuations.

During a recession, the national debt tends to rise sharply. Lower tax receipts from a depressed economy and higher spending via automatic stabilizers—such as unemployment insurance—push deficits higher. Actions to reduce a downturn in the business cycle, such as government spending, stimulus packages, or tax cuts to stimulate business, further exacerbate the deficit situation.

The following business cycle chart (Table A-1) shows the duration of peaks (the highs of the economy) and troughs (the lows of the economy), and the length of business cycles dating back to 1854.

Table A-1. Business Cycle Expansions and Contractions (duration in months)

	Contraction	Expansion	Cycle	
	Peak to trough	Previous trough to this peak	Trough from previous trough	Peak from previous peak
Average, all cycles				
1854–2009 (33 cycles)	16	42	56	55*
1854–1919 (16 cycles)	22	27	48	49**
1919–1945 (6 cycles)	18	35	53	53
1945–2009 (11 cycles)	11	59	73	66

*32 cycles.
**15 cycles.
Source: National Bureau of Economic Research, Business Cycle Expansions and Contractions.

Some cycles have been strong and long, such as the Great Depression, which ran for 43 months and resulted in a global economic collapse. Other downturn cycles have been relatively modest and quick, such as the shortest contraction in history which lasted just 6 months, from January 1980 to July 1980.

The chart shows the average recession (contraction) has shortened over time, and the average expansion has lengthened over time. The most recent grouping shows there have been 11 business cycles post-World War II (1945–2009). The average recession lasts just 11 months, and the typical expansion is 59 months. Another way to think about this is that the tough times last for close to a year, but the good times roll for almost 5 years.

The most recent recession was called in December 2007. Many economists and business people say this has been the toughest recession since the Great Depression. This contraction was officially called to an end in June 2009, by the Business Cycle Dating Committee of the National Bureau of Economic Research, for an 18-month-long recession. Still, the economic recovery since then has been weak at best. During the past few years, the government has taken in lower tax revenues as business income has faltered and as a result of the political decisions to cut taxes. The government has also initiated additional government spending policies in an attempt to stimulate demand. As discussed in the book, this has caused a widening gap—decreased revenues on one hand and increased spending on the other—causing the deficit to spiral.

Has there been too much effort put toward spending policies in an effort to stimulate the economy? Some, like economist Paul Krugman, would like to have seen even more spending as a means to create more jobs. Others say yes, given its negative impact on the deficit and the modest multiplier effects produced. As the economy matures, policymakers, along with the public, must be educated on the most effective use of fiscal (and monetary) tools to smooth out highs and lows in the economy.

The downturn has highlighted some flaws in the economy. In turn, they are teaching us valuable lessons related to the federal government:

- It is important for the government not to overextend. It must practice some level of fiscal austerity, or the debt can spiral out of control in a short time period, as we have witnessed.

- A political commitment from both parties will be necessary to put the debt under control. Many options are available—cutting spending, adjusting entitlement programs, or raising taxes—and political infighting must be put aside to place the economy on a strong path.

- Although fiscal and monetary policies are available to help dampen the economic cycles, it is not an exact science. During this recession, a host of monetary and fiscal programs were utilized. Policymakers are constantly learning from past mistakes and have a goal of reaching the optimal and most effective fiscal and monetary policies.

Missing from other books on the debt issue is what you can do if you feel it is important to reduce the deficit. Or perhaps you are merely interested in monitoring the level of the deficit and rising debt level.

Options are available to those who are interested in having a role in the fiscal environment. You do not need to be a policymaker to have an impact. The public can actually make contributions to the U.S. debt. More practically, we also can become educated taxpayers, exercise our right to vote, and submit ideas to our congressmen. Interested? Read on.

Make a Monetary Contribution

If you feel so inclined and are really concerned about the debt, you can "put your money where your mouth is." The Bureau of the Public Debt will accept gifts made on the premise that these funds are utilized to apply to the debt.

Gifts to reduce debt held by the public are usually made by concerned citizens. As you can see in the following chart, the total of these gifts typically run from $1 to $3 million a year. At this point, it's not enough to have a huge impact in the reduction of debt, but it does make a statement that citizens are concerned and fearful of the burgeoning debt. After all, the contributions are totally voluntary.

Table A-2. Contributions to Reduce the Federal Debt

Fiscal Year to Date	Total
2011	$3,277,369.23
2010	2,840,466.75
2009	3,063,057.05
2008	2,189,358.89
2007	2,624,862.42
2006	1,646,209.41
2005	1,455,541.65
2004	664,911.25
2003	1,277,423.40
2002	744,675.06
2001	1,645,082.28
2000	1,868,891.93

Source: Bureau of the Public Debt.

The chart shows that over the past 10 years, the Bureau of the Public Debt has seen a substantial increase in payments. There was a low point in 2004, with about $665 thousand, but the dollar amount hit over $3 million in 2011. These figures include, along with citizen contributions, monies that have been left by individuals to the Bureau of the Public Debt from their estates after they died.

You can make a contribution online using a credit card, checking, or savings account, and it is very easy. The government has instructions at http://pay.gov.

Do you prefer snail mail? Simply write a check payable to the Bureau of the Public Debt, and note that it's a "gift to reduce the debt held by the public." Mail your check to this address:

Attn. Dept G
Bureau of the Public Debt
P.O. Box 2188
Parkersburg, WV 26106–2188.

Become an Educated Taxpayer

It is important to remember that you are a U.S. taxpayer and this is your government. You need to take action and responsibility to ensure that your government fulfills its roles and responsibilities in a manner that reflects your beliefs. The future of the United States, the world's economic power-house, is important to each and every one of us. If you are interested in helping build and sustain a stronger fiscal environment, there are options available to make an impact.

Although one individual citizen may have only a small influence, the combined efforts of all 314,316,802 U.S. residents can be forceful. Just imagine if every person in the United States took one action step. Simple steps will make a difference. You have the power to potentially alter the course of the economy and the nation's future for your children and your children's children.

Take time to research and learn about the current debt and deficit issues. Reading this book has been a good start. The Internet (resources are listed in Appendix B), television, newspapers, and social media are packed full of government budget, deficit, and debt information.

Attend a political party event, a government spending forum, or any educational seminars. Exchange ideas with friends and family on the proper fiscal role for the federal government. Be a spokesperson and share your knowledge of the deficit/debt situation with others. Let others learn from you.

Don't forget the social media. It is a powerful tool for instantaneously exchanging information and reaching the masses in a matter of minutes.

Be sure to monitor the debt situation on a regular basis. Government spending, taxation, and the budget are issues that can change quickly. Don't let the material become stagnate. Stay on top of one of the most pertinent issues of our times.

■ **Tip** Here's a way for you to get an idea of the trade-offs necessary if we are ever to eliminate the deficit. Visit this web site and fix the budget deficit as you see fit: www.nytimes.com/ interactive/2010/11/13/weekinreview/deficits-graphic.html.

Vote

The best way to let your voice be heard on matters of the national debt is by using your vote wisely. Pay attention to candidates and their views on taxation, government spending, the deficit, and the national debt. Does the candidate have the same fiscal stance as you do? Look at the candidate's platform and past record on budgetary issues.

Attend political forums and debates. Ask the tough questions: How might you reduce the debt? Do you think taxes should be raised or lowered? If you are elected, how might you adjust the new budgetary proposal? Do you believe the debt has been brought under control?

Contact Your Senator or Congressman

If you have a specific idea or concern about the deficit issue, be sure to contact your U.S. senator or state representative. You can also comment on current or pending legislation and public policy issues.

Your letter should be written to deliver clear, well-researched points. A bullet-point format is visually appealing, easy to read, and useful for emphasizing concerns. Keeping the letter brief and professional will be an attention-grabber.

Following is the address for sending snail mail to your senator:

The Honorable (Name)
United States Senate
Washington, DC 20510

You may also e-mail a U.S. senator by logging on to the U.S. Senate website at www.senate.gov and clicking Senators to find the ones from your state. When e-mailing your senator, you'll need to include your return mail address and e-mail address.

To contact your state representatives, go to http://writerep.house.gov or www.congress.org. By merely plugging in your ZIP code, you will find a listing of your representatives. If you prefer snail mail, write to this address:

U.S. Representative
The Honorable (Name)
U.S. House of Representatives
Washington, DC 20515

Remember that simple steps taken by many will help build a fiscally strong foundation for the U.S. economy. Appendix B follows with more Internet resources to assist in your educational journey.

Websites for Debt and Deficit Information

This appendix lists Internet resources for more information about the U.S. debt and deficit. The resources are divided into two categories: government agencies and private organizations.

Government Agencies

www.publicdebt.treas.gov

The Bureau of the Public Debt is a small agency within the Treasury Department. The role of the Bureau is to borrow funds for the operation of the federal government and to account for the resulting debt.

In 1776, a committee of ten founders took the helm of what would later become the Treasury. The group obtained money for the United States from the governments of France and The Netherlands, via a form of bonds called *loan certificates*. The details found on this website provide a fascinating look at the early financial history of our republic.

www.treasurydirect.gov

The U.S. Department of the Treasury Bureau of the Public Debt brings the public the TreasuryDirect website. TreasuryDirect is the first and only financial services website that lets you buy and redeem securities directly from the U.S. Department of the Treasury in paperless electronic form.

You can spend hours perusing this jam-packed website. Take a look at the details on T-bills, notes and bonds, and savings bonds. Get an update by taking a look at the monthly statement of the public debt. For the super inquisitive, learn how Treasury auctions work. The well-known "debt to the penny" is updated daily so you can keep a pulse on the current debt situation.

www.whitehouse.gov/omb

The Office of Management and Budget (OMB) is part of the Executive Office of the President of the United States. The OMB's main role is to assist the president in overseeing the preparation of the federal budget and supervising the administration of executive branch agencies.

The historical information is top-notch. The site provides data on budget receipts, outlays, surpluses or deficits, debt, and federal employment—largely from 1940 or earlier, up to 2017. Explore some of the specific pages on this site, such as the President's budget, fact sheets on key issues, and past budgets.

www.cbo.gov

The Congressional Budget Office (CBO) is an agency of Congress. It is the role of the CBO to provide Congress with impartial, objective analyses for economic and budget decisions, along with estimates to assist in the Congressional budget process.

Be sure to read the reports required for the budget process, "The Budget and Economic Outlook," and "An Analysis of the President's Budget." For a short, quick summary of the topics related to budgetary analysis, check out the always insightful Director's Blog by Douglas W. Elmendorf, the eighth director of CBO. A must read is the "Monthly Budget Review," which details government fiscal activity for the month. On the main page, you can sign up for e-mail from the CBO, which will always keep you up-to-date on releases of new documents, new advisories, and job announcements.

www.fiscalcommission.gov

President Obama set up a bipartisan group called the National Commission on Fiscal Responsibility and Reform to find ways to address the country's fiscal challenges, specifically to deal with the rising debt. Cochaired by former Republican Senator Alan Simpson and former Clinton White House Chief of Staff Erskine Bowles, the meetings of the commission can be viewed by clicking "Meetings."

In December 2010, the group published a 59-page report titled "Moment of Truth: Report on the National Commission of Fiscal Responsbility and Reform." It is a fascinating, detailed plan to reduce the deficit to the tune of almost $4 trillion through 2020. Be sure to check out the tough discretionary spending cuts, the tax-reform plan, and cuts to Social Security.

Private Organizations

www.cagw.org

Citizens Against Government Waste (CAGW) refers to itself as "America's Number #1 Taxpayer Watchdog." Located in Washington, DC, CAGW is a private, nonpartisan, nonprofit entity that touts over one million members. The mission of the organization is to "eliminate waste, mismanagement, and inefficiency in the federal government."

On the home page, you can sign up to be an online member of the organization, and receive the monthly newsletter and action alerts. The organization is well-known for *The Congressional Pig Book*, available online. It is an annual listing of the pork-barrel projects in the federal budget.

You will find many crazy pork spending "awards" listed by specific year, from 1991 through 2012. For example, the 2010 Do You Want Fries with That Award: $2,573,000 for potato research in four states, requested by five senators and five representatives. Or check out the Sapping the Taxpayers Award: $4.8 million for wood utilization research in 11 states, requested by 13 senators and 10 representatives. In 2012, $5,000,000 went to an abstinence education program that was not even requested by the Department of Education.

www.concordcoalition.org

Founded in 1992, The Concord Coalition is a nonpartisan, nonprofit, grassroots organization based in Arlington, Virginia. The mission of the organization is stated as "dedicated to educating the public about the causes and consequences of federal budget deficits, the long-term challenges facing America's unsustainable entitlement programs, and how to build a sound foundation for economic growth." The Concord Coalition believes informed voters will require fiscal responsibility of their elected leaders.

Featured on the website are several must-see areas: Key Questions Voters Should Ask Candidates, Fiscal Wakeup Tours, Fiscal Solutions Tour, a detailed

Issues section, and search capability for an extensive array of publications. Be sure to click the "Act" section for a wide variety of opportunities for those interested in fiscal control. It has an extensive breadth of information for fiscally inquisitive citizens. Scroll through the main tabs: Washington Budget Report, Publications, Principles and Priorities Online, The Tabulation Blog, and Highlights and Favorites.

www.heritage.org

The Heritage Foundation, founded in 1973, is located in Washington, DC, and it has been very influential in public policy. This conservative think tank has a mission to "formulate and promote conservative public policies based on the principles of free enterprise, limited government, individual freedom, traditional American values, and a strong national defense." The organization is nonprofit, supported by more than 710,000 individual, foundation, and corporate donors.

The wide variety of research, budget, and spending information is top-notch. Check out " U.S. Debt Hits $16 Trillion," the blogpost published on September 4, 2012, by Romina Boccia, Research Coordinator for Domestic and Economic Policy. Or read an Issue Briefing from David Addington, Heritage's vice president for Domestic and Economic Policy, published March 14, 2012, entitled "Federal Budget: What Congress Must Do to Control Spending and Create Jobs."

This website/think tank offers insightful reading and will help you get a handle on a wide variety of debt, deficit, and budgetary issues. On the main web page, you can sign up via e-mail for Heritage's updates on current events and initiatives.

www.urban.org

The Washington, DC-based Urban Institute is a nonpartisan economic and social research center. This organization, founded in 1968, "gathers data, conducts research, evaluates programs, offers technical assistance overseas, and educates Americans on social and economic issues—to foster sound public policy and effective government."

View the Economy and Taxes section, and you will find a multitude of publications dealing with proposals to control deficits and reform the entitlement programs. For a quick overview of the deficit issue, be sure to read "Five Questions: Robert Reischauer, on Reining in Massive Federal Deficits." Reischauer, president of Urban Institute, advocates enacting legislation soon to slow the growth of spending and increase taxes. Want more? Read on to "Five Questions: Donald Marron on Cutting Tax Preferences As the Key to

Tax Reform." Marron, director of the Tax Policy Center, educates the reader on redesigning tax preferences, noting "many of which are spending programs in disguise."

www.nber.org

The National Bureau of Economic Research (NBER) is a private, nonpartisan, not-for-profit economic research organization. This organization, based in Cambridge, Massachusetts, is "dedicated to promoting a greater understanding of how the economy works." NBER has more than 1,000 professors of economics and business who teach and conduct research as NBER researchers. They work on a wide variety of issues that confront our society. High-quality research and working papers are produced by this select group.

As a plus, the NBER's Business Cycle Dating Committee maintains a chronology of the U.S. business cycle back to 1854. This is the place to research the historical data on business cycle recessions and expansions. NBER's Business Cycle Dating Committee also provides information about how it chooses the turning points in the economy. Under Data, click "Business Cycle Memos," and you will find a plethora of information about recessions and recoveries. For those who want to be educated in historical trends as well as the current cycle, this is the place to be. If you would like to receive immediate notice of the announcements of the NBER Business Cycle Dating Committee by e-mail, you may register your e-mail address.

Read on to Appendix C to get a glimpse into the blueprint plans of both major parties, Republican and Democratic, to tame the debt. Fiscal policies have been around for years and this appendix provides and overview of deficit plans by presidential administrations. As you can see, sometimes fiscal policies work and sometimes they fail miserably.

APPENDIX

C

Political Party Views of the Debt

The political issue of the day, for both parties, is the faltering economy; and at the top of the list of economic issues—the runaway debt. Who is to blame for the massive $16 trillion debt and the foreboding $1 trillion plus deficits? Both political parties share some culpability.

Political Parties' Plans to Reduce the Debt and Deficit

While Republicans and Democrats both express grave concern over the debt, attempts at compromise have largely failed. If an agreeable plan cannot be implemented to tame the debt, then beginning in 2013, automatic spending cuts take effect. The spending cuts are expected to achieve about $1.2 trillion in savings over 10 years, divided equally between defense and many domestic programs. We no longer have the luxury of playing the blame game. We must work together on some type of compromise, likely involving a mix of decreased spending, increased taxes, and entitlement reforms.

As a step toward this goal, in February 2010, President Obama created an 18-member bipartisan commission to work on a solution. It is called the National Commission on Fiscal Responsibility and Reform, and is often referred to as Simpson-Bowles, named after cochairs former Republican Senator Alan Simpson and former Democratic White House Chief of Staff Erskine Bowles. The President created the bipartisan commission to improve the fiscal situation in the medium term and to achieve fiscal sustainability over the long run, or to find ways to reduce the mounting debt. Later that year the commission's report was released as a plan to combine spending cuts and tax increases. While overwhelming support existed, it did not receive the supermajority 14 votes needed to send it to Congress for a vote. Still Simpson-Bowles may be used as a model for a potential deal in the future.

A major missed opportunity came in July 2011, when negotiations between President Obama and Republican Speaker of the House John Boehner ceased. Reportedly, the negotiations—commonly referred to as the "grand bargain"— to raise the debt limit included a major package that would have cut spending by $3.5 trillion over the next 10 years. It included a major overhaul of the budget process, increased tax revenues, and entitlement reforms. The two were close to making a deal, and although reports vary on the reason, Boehner made a decision to leave the negotiations. Whisperings have the President trying to change the deal at the last minute to demand additional revenue through tax increases.

Philosophical Underpinnings

A political novice might wonder what the difficulty is in coming to a compromise. We all make concessions on a daily basis—with people at work, school, church, and at home. The challenge for politicians is that each of the major parties, Republicans and Democrats, comes from different stances or philosophies, which makes it a challenge.

Republicans are viewed as the conservative party. They tend to support a limited government and are probusiness. Republicans generally believe that encouraging private individuals and businesses can be more productive for society and can improve the country's economic growth. And as such, they are against an excessive level of government bureaucracy and red tape. Competition and self-reliance can improve our economy and society. As a rule, Republicans are in favor of cutting government spending, and this includes spending on entitlement programs and not increasing taxes. The party tends to support tax cuts across the board, at all economic levels. They are particularly adamant against tax increases for the wealthy.

The Democratic Party is seen as more liberal. Democrats generally support big government and are strong advocates protecting the entitlement programs. The party maintains that society and individuals can be bettered and life enriched with governmental involvement. Everyone should get a fair chance, and government should work for the common good of all. Democrats favor higher taxation of the wealthy to generate revenue. The party champions government spending, particularly in the entitlement area, and is greatly interested in protecting Social Security, Medicare, Medicaid, and other social programs.

It is a fact that each party will need to give on some of its long-held beliefs to reach an agreement to reduce the deficit. The Republican side must give on tax issues, and the Democratic side will need to retreat on entitlement program spending. Hence, we have the basic formula that will reduce the deficit—an increase in taxes and a reduction in spending. The next president—Republican or Democrat—will need to take charge of the bipartisan negotiations and reduce the deficit, for the good of our country.

Incumbent Democratic President Barack Obama favors allowing the Bush-era tax cuts to expire as well as limiting deductions for high earners. His recent budget did contain over $5 trillion in deficit reduction measures over 5 years, but there was not much give on the entitlement side. Republican presidential candidate Mitt Romney believes in capping federal spending at 20 percent of GDP by 2016, overhauling the tax code, repealing the Patient Protection and Affordable Care Act—ObamaCare—and reducing individual and corporate tax rates to stimulate our economy. Romney wants to develop cost savings by giving more control to the states via a block-grant program, and allowing states to innovate in such areas as Medicaid and worker retraining.

PAUL RYAN

On August 11, 2012, Republican presidential candidate Mitt Romney announced Paul Ryan as his vice presidential running mate. Ryan, age 42 years, is a U.S. Representative from Wisconsin and the Party's leader on fiscal reforms. As the chairman of the House Budget Committee, Ryan has proposed cost-cutting entitlement program reforms in an effort to reduce the U.S. debt.

Ryan's proposals have come under severe scrutiny from Democrats, who generally favor tax hikes for the wealthy, tax cuts on the middle class, and protecting entitlement programs. The Democratic Party maintains that Ryan's plan will harm the poor and destroy Medicare. The Republicans contend that the plan will curtail out-of-control spending. This plan would cut spending by $6 trillion over 10 years, while President Obama's plan proposes to cut $4 trillion in spending over 12 years.

The most controversial part of Ryan's plan relates to the restructuring of Medicare, the health insurance program for seniors. Ryan proposes leaving traditional Medicare for those currently 55 and over, but privatizing Medicare for younger people. Sometimes referred to as a voucher program, Ryan proposes giving people a subsidy to buy their own health insurance. This would shift additional cost to beneficiaries.

Medicaid and food stamps would be turned into block grant programs under this proposal, giving states a lump sum. Individual states would have large discretion on how to spend the funds.

The plan also calls for a tax code overhaul to the complicated system, eliminating many tax breaks, and having only two individual tax rates—10 percent and 25 percent. Ryan projects his budget to balance by the year 2040, followed by surpluses.

Track Record

Generally, you will find that presidents tend to toe the party line, but some do diverge. Independent thinking, for the good of our country, is needed. The following is a quick look over the past 50 years to see what our presidential administrations have done regarding taxes, spending, and the deficit situation. You will find some determined, analytical thinkers.

President	Party	Term of Office
John F. Kennedy	Democrat	1961–1963

Debt Action: JFK went against traditional Democratic lines and cut taxes to stimulate the economy. It was a successful action. The top marginal tax rates were dropped along with capital gains, and as a result, federal tax revenues actually rose.

Lyndon Johnson	Democrat	1963–1969

Debt Action: Taking a traditional Democratic stance, Johnson's Great Society entitlement programs were largely acclaimed and successful, but the deficit spiked. Spending on the Vietnam War also intensified the deficit.

Richard Nixon	Republican	1969–1974

Debt Action: Nixon accepted deficit spending to stimulate the sluggish economy. He stepped away from the traditional Republican Party stance of balanced budgets to deal with the turbulent and sagging economy of the early 1970s.

Gerald Ford	Republican	1974–1977

Debt Action: Ford represented the Republican Party by reducing spending on many social programs. He was well-known for battling Congress, using his veto power to tame spending, and keeping the economy on track. He was wary of budget deficits and even opposed a permanent tax cut because he was concerned about its long-term impact on deficits.

President	Party	Term of Office
Jimmy Carter	Democrat	1977–1981

Debt Action: Carter attempted to control spending and early on he pledged to eliminate deficits. Even though deficits rose during his term in office, he did make some tough decisions and cut spending in some major Democratic programs.

Ronald Reagan	Republican	1981–1989

Debt Action: While Republican Ronald Reagan was in office the national debt hit $1 trillion. The Reagan era is well-known for supply side economics—cutting tax rates to stimulate the economy and generate revenue. It was held that the budget could be balanced using this tactic. The economy thrived, but so did the debt. When Reagan left office the debt was near $3 trillion.

George H. W. Bush	Republican	1989–1993

Debt Action: George H. W. Bush compromised, accepting a tax increase along with spending cuts to reduce the deficit. He went against his platform promise of "no new taxes" for the good of the country.

William J. Clinton	Democrat	1993–2001

Debt Action: The last 3 years of the Clinton administration saw surpluses, the last we have seen to the time of this writing. Some suggest that Clinton was the recipient of a burgeoning economy and peaking stock market. But early on in 1993, Clinton did toe party line with an increase in taxes on high wage earners.

George W. Bush	Republican	2001–2009

Debt Action: Republican George W. Bush is well-known for the Bush tax cuts, a very Republican line. Bush-era tax cuts, also known as the Economic Growth and Tax Relief Reconciliation Act of 2001, lowered the marginal tax rates for virtually all individuals and families. In addition, the Jobs and Growth Tax Relief Reconciliation Act of 2003 accelerated the cuts and added reductions in capital gains and dividends. These were designed as temporary measures to promote long-term growth because incentives were realigned and people would be encouraged to work more. But debate exists over the effectiveness of the tax cuts. Ultimately, the economy sagged, recessions hit in 2001 and 2007, and deficits rose.

President	Party	Term of Office
Barack Obama	Democrat	2009–present

Debt Action: Obama passed the $787 billion economic stimulus bill in 2009, American Recovery and Reinvestment Act, to recharge the economy. Stimulating the economy was justified, but most of the stimulus spending ended after 2010. Most say the effect of the bill was modest at best—modest effects on employment and output. The CBO maintains the results of the stimulus spending were gone after 2011. The deficit, due to the impact of stimulus spending and the depressed revenues thanks to the "Great Recession," has increased substantially.

Bibliography

Austin, D. Andrew, and Levit, Mindy R. "The Debt Limit: History and Recent Increases," January 28, 2010 (Congressional Research Service Report No. RL31967). Available at http://opencrs.com/document/RL31967/2010-01-28/ (accessed May 28, 2011). Bank of America. "Form 10-K for fiscal year ended December 31, 2011"). Available at www.sec.gov (accessed July 30, 2012).

Bernanke, Ben S. *The Crisis and the Policy Response,* speech delivered at the Stamp Lecture, London School of Economics, London, England, January 13, 2009. Available at www.federalreserve.gov/newsevents/speech/bernanke20090113a.htm (accessed February 16, 2011).

Bernanke, Ben S. *Semiannual Monetary Policy Report to the Congress*, speech delivered before the Committee on Banking, Housing, and Urban Affairs, U.S. Senate, Washington, DC, July 17, 2012, www.federalreserve.gov/newsevents/testimony/bernanke20120717a.htm (Accessed July 23, 2012).

Blackwell, Ken, and Klukowski, Ken. *The Huffington Post.* "Hatch and Lee's Balanced Budget Amendment: A Win for America," April 1, 2011. Available at www.huffingtonpost.com (accessed May 23, 2011).

The Board of Trustees, Federal Old-Age and Survivors Insurance and Federal Disability Insurance Trust Funds. *The 2011 Annual Report of the Board of Trustees of the Federal Old-Age and Survivors Insurance and Federal Disability Insurance Trust Funds*, May 13, 2011. Washington, D.C.: U.S. Government Printing Office. Available at www.ssa.gov/oact/TR/2011/ (accessed June 16, 2011).

Board of Trustees. *The 2012 Annual Report of the Board of Trustees of the Federal Old-Age and Survivors Insurance and Federal Disability Insurance Trust Funds*, April 25, 2012. Washington, DC: Government Printing Office. Available at www.ssa.gov (accessed September 10, 2012).

Bureau of the Public Debt. "Commissioner's Welcome." Available at www.publicdebt.treas.gov/whoweare/welcome.htm (accessed February 8, 2011).

Bureau of the Public Debt. "Our History." Available at www.publicdebt.treas.gov/history/history.htm (accessed February 6, 2011).

Bussing-Burks, Marie. *Money for Minors: A Student's Guide to Economics.* Westport, CT: Greenwood Publishing Group. 2008.

Clement, Scott. "Tea Party Support Stable, but Interest Is Waning," April 15, 2012. Available at http://www.washingtonpost.com/blogs/behind-the-numbers/post/tea-party-support-stable-but-interest-is-waning/2012/04/14/gIQAPXyKHT_blog.html.

Citizens Against Government Waste. *2010 Congressional Pig Book Summary.* Washington, DC. Available at www.cagw.org/reports/pig-book/2010/ (accessed May 14, 2011 and May 28, 2011).

Citizens Against Government Waste, 2012 Congressional Pig Book Summary, Washington, D.C. Available at www.cagw.org/reports/pig-book/2012/ (accessed September 15, 2012).

Coburn, Tom. *Wastebook 2010:* A Guide to Some of the Most Wasteful Government Spending of 2010, December 2010. Available at http://www.coburn.senate.gov/public//index.cfm?a=Files.Serve&File_id=4a184ddb-cd85-4052-b38b-5a1116acca8c (accessed May 27, 2011).

The Concord Coalition. "About the Concord Coalition." Available at www.concordcoalition.org/about-concord-coalition (accessed March 27, 2011).

Congressional Budget Office. *The Budget and Economic Outlook: Fiscal Years 2012 to 2022,* January 2012. Available at www.cbo.gov/publication/43539.

Congressional Budget Office. *Estimated Impact of the American Recovery and Reinvestment Act on Employment and Economic Output from October 2010 Through December 2010,* February 2011. Available at www.cbo.gov (accessed February 27, 2011).

Congressional Budget Office. *Estimated Impact of the American Recovery and Reinvestment Act on Employment and Economic Output from April 2012 Through June 2012,* August 2012. Available at www.cbo.gov (accessed September 12, 2012).

Congressional Budget Office. *Federal Debt and the Risk of a Fiscal Crisis,* July 27, 2010. Available at www.cbo.gov/doc.cfm?index=11659 (accessed May 17, 2011).

Congressional Budget Office. *Reducing the Deficit: Spending and Revenue Options,* March 2011. Available at www.cbo.gov/doc.cfm?index=12085 (accessed May 27, 2011).

Economic Policy Institute. "Over 1,000 Economists Oppose Balanced Budget Amendment, Warning It Is 'Unsound and Unnecessary,'" news release. Available at www.ombwatch.org/files/bba/econ.html (accessed June 21, 2011).

The Eleanor Roosevelt Papers. "The Great Depression," *Teaching Eleanor Roosevelt,* edited by Allida Black, June Hopkins, et al. (Hyde Park, NY: Eleanor Roosevelt National Historic Site, 2003). Available at www.gwu.edu/~erpapers/teachinger/glossary/great-depression.cfm (accessed September 15, 2012).

The Federal Reserve. "Federal Reserve Statistical Release G.19: 'Consumer Credit,'" September 10, 2012. Available at www.federalreserve.gov/releases/g19/current/default.htm (accessed September 15, 2012).

Federal Reserve Board of Governors. "G19, Consumer Credit," Federal Reserve Statistical Release, March 2011. Available at www.federalreserve.gov (accessed May 14, 2011).

Full Employment and Balanced Growth Act of 1978, 15 USC § 3101 (1978).

Gorman, Tom. *The Complete Idiot's Guide to Economics.* New York, NY: Penguin Group, 2003.

Hoag, Arleen J., and Hoag, John H. *Introductory Economics, 2nd edition.* Englewood Cliffs, NJ: Prentice Hall, Inc., 1991.

Hubbard, R. Glenn, and O'Brien, Anthony Patrick. *Macroeconomics, 3rd edition.* Boston, MA: Pearson Education, Inc., 2010.

International Labour Organization. *2012 World of Work Report: Summary.* Available at www.ilo.org (accessed July 27, 2012).

International Monetary Fund. United States: Selected Issues Paper, "IMF Country Report No. 10/248," July 2010. Washington, DC. Available at www.imf.org (accessed February 27, 2011).

International Monetary Fund. "World Economic Outlook Update," July 16, 2012. Available at www.imf.org (accessed July 30, 2012).

Library of Congress/Thomas. Bill Summary & Status, "95th Congress (1977–1978). H.R. 50: Full Employment and Balanced Growth Act." Available at http://thomas.loc.gov (accessed February 19, 2011).

Miller, Roger LeRoy. The Macro View, 16th edition. Boston, MA: Pearson Education, Inc., 2012.

Moody's. "'AAA/A-1+' Rating on United States of America Affirmed; Outlook Revised to Negative," September 11, 2012. Available at http://www.moodys.com/research/Moodys-issues-update-on-the-outlook-for-the-US-governments--PR_254944 (accessed September 15, 2012).

National Bureau of Economic Research. "Announcement of June 2009 Business Cycle Through/End of Last Recession, September 20, 2010." Available at www.nber.org (accessed April 25, 2010).

National Bureau of Economic Research. "Business Cycle Dating Committee, National Bureau of Economic Research report," September 20, 2010. Available at www.nber.org/cycles/sept2010.html (accessed April 25, 2011).

National Foundation for Credit Counseling. *The 2011 Consumer Financial Literacy Survey, Final Report,* March 2011. Washington, DC. Prepared by Harris Interactive Inc. Public Relations Research. Available at www.ncff.org (accessed May 14, 2011).

The National Foundation for Credit Counseling and the Network Branded Prepaid Card Association. *The 2012 Consumer Financial Literacy Survey, Final Report,* April 2012 (prepared by Harris Interactive Inc. Public Relations Research). Available at www.nfcc.org/NewsRoom/newsreleases/SIGNIFICANT_GAPS.cfm (accessed September 15, 2012).

National Parks Service. "The Great Depression (1929–1939)." Eleanor Roosevelt National Historic Site. Available at www.nps.gov (accessed March 20, 2011).

Office of Management and Budget. Budget of the U.S. Government, Fiscal Year 2011. Available at www.budget.gov (accessed February 4, 2011).

Office of Management and Budget. Budget of the U.S. Government, Fiscal Year 2012. Available at www.budget.gov (accessed May 1, 2011).

Organisation for Economic Co-operation and Development. "Economic Outlook 91," Press Conference, Paris, May 22, 2012. Available at www.oecd.org (accessed July 30, 2012).

Organisation for Economic Co-operation and Development, "Government debt", *Economics: Key Tables from OECD,* No. 21, 2012. doi: 10.1787/gov-debt-table-2012-1-en.

Page, Benjamin, and Reichling, Felix. "Macroeconomic Analysis: Estimated Impact of the American Recovery and Reinvestment Act on Employment and Economic Output from October 2010 Through December 2010," Congressional Budget Office Director's Blog, February 23, 2011. Available at http://cboblog.cbo.gov/?p=1852 (accessed February 24, 2011).

Parkin, Michael. *Macroeconomics, 10th edition.* Boston, MA: Pearson Education, 2012.

Pennington, Robert L. *Economics.* Austin, TX: Holt, Rinehart and Winston, 1999.

Politico. "Unsustainable Budget Threatens Nation," March 24, 2011. Available at www.politico.com/news/stories/0311/51864.html (accessed May 16, 2011).

Rooney, Ben. "U.S. Credit Rating Outlook Lowered by S&P," April 19, 2011. Available at CNNMoney.com (accessed May 17, 2011).

Ryan, Paul. "The Path to Prosperity: Restoring America's Promise, Fiscal Year 2012 Budget Resolution," Report to House Committee on the Budget. Available at budget.house.gov (accessed June 24, 2011).

Saad, Lydia. "Americans Believe GOP Should Consider Tea Party Ideas," January 31, 2011. Available at www.gallup.com (accessed March 25, 2011).

Saad, Lydia. "Federal Debt, Terrorism Considered Top Threats to U.S.," June 4, 2010. Available at www.gallup.com (accessed February 4, 2011).

Social Security Administration. *Fast Facts and Figures about Social Security.* Available at www.ssa.gov (accessed September 10, 2012).

Social Security Administration. *Social Security Basic Facts.* Available at www.ssa.gov (accessed June 28, 2011).

Standard & Poor's. "'AAA/A-1+' Rating on United States of America Affirmed; Outlook Revised to Negative." April 18, 2011. Available at www.standardandpoors.com (accessed May 17, 2011).

Standard & Poor's. "Global Potential Downgrades: An Increase Globally Following the Outlook Revisions to Negative for the U.S. and Japan," May 9, 2011. Available at www.standardandpoors.com (accessed May 17, 2011).

Standard & Poors. "United States of America Long-Term Rating Lowered to 'AA+' Political Risks, Rising Debt Burden, Outlook Negative," August 5, 2011. Available at www.standardandpoors.com/ratings/articles/en/us/?assetID=1245316529563 (accessed September 17, 2012).

Suskind, Ron. *The Price of Loyalty.* New York, NY: Simon & Schuster, 2004.

TreasuryDirect. "Interest Expense on the Debt Outstanding." Available at www.treasurydirect.gov (accessed February 5, 2011).

TreasuryDirect Kids. "The Basics of Treasury Securities." Available at www.treasurydirect.gov (accessed February 6, 2011).

TreasuryDirect Kids. "The History of the Public Debt: The New Deal (1933-1936) to World War II (1939-1945)." Available at www.treasurydirect.gov (accessed February 6, 2011).

TreasuryDirect Kids. "The History of U.S. Public Debt: The Beginning of U.S. Debt." Available at www.treasurydirect.gov/kids/history/history.htm (accessed February 6, 2011).

TreasuryDirect Kids. "How Treasuries Work." Available at www.treasurydirect.gov (accessed February 6, 2011).

U.S. Census Bureau. *Statistical Abstract of the United States, 2011*, U.S. Census Bureau: Department of Commerce. Available at www.census.gov/compendia/statab/2011/2011edition.html (accessed June 16, 2011).

U.S. Department of the Treasury. *Annual Report on the Public Debt, Fiscal Year Ending on September 30, 2009*, Title 31, 3130, June 2010. Washington, DC. Department of the Treasury.

U.S. Department of the Treasury. "Statement of Treasury Assistant Secretary for Financial Markets Mary Miller on Credit Rating Agency Announcements Today," news release, April 18, 2011. Available at www.treasury.gov (accessed May 17, 2011).

U.S. Department of the Treasury Financial Management Service. Final Monthly Treasury Statement of Receipts and Outlays of the United States Government, for Fiscal Year 2010 through September 30, 2010, and other periods. Available at www.fms.treas.gov (accessed February 5, 2010).

Wessels, Walter. *Barron's Economics, 4th edition*. Hauppauge, NY: Barron's Educational Series, Inc., 2006.

World Trade Organization. 2012 Press Releases/658, April 12, 2012, World Trade 2011, Prospects for 2012. Available at www.wto.org (accessed July 25, 2012).

Zeck, Van. Bureau of the Public Debt. "Commissioner's Welcome," October 8, 2008. Available at www.publicdebt.treas.gov (accessed February 8, 2011).

I

Index

CPSIA information can be obtained at www.ICGtesting.com
Printed in the USA
LVOW120200011112

305358LV00003B/1/P